Jump Start Guide for Microsoft® Visual Basic® 2005

by Martin Schray

THOMSON
COURSE TECHNOLOGY

Australia • Canada • Mexico • Singapore • Spain • United Kingdom • United States

Jump Start Guide for Microsoft® Visual Basic® 2005

by Martin Schray

Executive Editor:
Bob Woodbury

Managing Editor:
William Pitkin III

Senior Product Manager:
Tricia Boyle

Associate Product Manager:
Sarah Santoro

Product Marketing Manager:
Brian Berkeley

Editorial Assistant:
Allison Murphy

Production Editor:
Jill Klaffky

Cover Designer:
Steve Deschene

Compositor:
GEX Publishing Services

Quality Assurance Coordinator:
Chris Scriver

Copy Editor:
Mark Goodin

Proofreader:
Susan Gall

Indexer:
Liz Cunningham

Printed in the United States of America

1 2 3 4 5 6 7 8 9 CS 08 07 06 05

For more information, contact Course Technology, 25 Thomson Place, Boston, Massachusetts, 02210.

Or find us on the World Wide Web at *www.course.com*.

ISBN 1-4188-3624-9

BRIEF

Contents

TABLE OF

Contents

Dedication

To my wonderful wife, Milanka; thanks for supporting me in all my endeavors. To my daughter, Alexandra, you are an inspiration to our family.

Preface

Jump Start Guide for Microsoft Visual Basic 2005 is written for Microsoft Visual Basic .NET 2003 developers (students, faculty, and professionals) who want to move to Microsoft Visual Basic 2005 and effectively use the new capabilities of Visual Basic 2005. The goal of this text is to allow you to quickly and easily build upon your existing Visual Basic .NET 2003 knowledge to get the most from Visual Basic 2005. There are a huge number of improvements that have been made in Visual Basic 2005. One change is that the name was simplified to Visual Basic 2005, rather then Visual Basic .NET 2005. It is useful to break down the large set of enhancements in Microsoft Visual Studio 2005 and Visual Basic 2005. For the most part, the enhancements can be grouped into the following three logical areas. This makes it easier to look at the full scope of the changes in Visual Studio 2005 and Visual Basic 2005.

(1) Enhancements to Visual Studio

- (a) These are additional features, capabilities, and entirely new designers that have been added to the Visual Studio 2005 Integrated Development Environment (IDE).
- (b) These changes allow you to design, edit, debug, and build your Visual Basic 2005 applications with improved speed and precision.

(2) Enhancements to the Visual Basic Language

- (a) These are changes, enhancements, and additions to the Visual Basic 2005 programming language.
- (b) These changes allow you to build your applications more quickly, with less code, and make some coding tasks much easier.

(3) Enhancements to Visual Basic Applications

- (a) These are additional features, capabilities, and new controls that have been added to Visual Basic 2005 that can be used when building windows forms, Web forms, and mobile applications.
- (b) These changes allow you to quickly build more powerful, interactive, and visually interesting applications.

This book allows you to make use of the new Visual Studio 2005 features, build powerful visual applications quickly, and use the new Visual Basic language features to get more done with less code!

Approach

This book is intended for two audiences: *academic* and *professional developers*. Those in the academic field can use this book in conjunction with a Visual Basic .NET 2003 textbook, such as one of the Visual Basic books offered by Thomson Course Technology. This book is meant to supplement these excellent texts and allows faculty to introduce and use new features in Viusal Basic 2005 as part of their course. Because this book is a supplement to a textbook, it does not include typical end-of-chapter materials.

Professional developers who have a solid base of experience using Visual Basic .NET 2003 and want to quickly begin using the new features in Viusal Basic 2005 will also benefit from this book.

After completing this book, readers will be able to effectively use the new features in Visual Studio 2005 and Visual Basic 2005 to build applications.

Organization and Coverage

Jump Start Guide for Microsoft Visual Basic 2005 covers the enhancements to Visual Studio 2005 as well as the language enhancements in Visual Basic 2005. It then looks at enhancements as they relate to building windows, Web, and mobile applications using Visual Basic 2005. Finally, the book covers accessing databases from Visual Basic 2005 using ADO.NET. Appendix A covers ClickOnce application deployment.

A short overview of each chapter and the appendix are provided here.

Chapter 1: Enhancements to Visual Studio 2005

This chapter covers the large number of enhancements that have been made to Visual Studio 2005 as they relate to designing, debugging and building Visual Basic 2005 applications, as well as writing code using the designers or the code editor. The Class Designer, Object Test Bench, debugger datatips, debugger visualizations, code snippets, and the return of edit and continue features make building applications easier and faster.

Chapter 2: Visual Basic 2005 Language Enhancements

This chapter covers the language enhancement in Visual Basic 2005. These enhancements can make application development easier, increase reuse, or just make life easier for you as you build your application. The new My. Capability feature makes writing Visual Basic code much easier without the user having to know a great deal about .NET Framework namespaces. The addition of new operators, operator overloading, application events, and generics make Visual Basic 2005 far more capabale then its predecesors.

Chapter 3: Enhancements to Windows Forms Application Development

This chapter discusses enhanced or new capabilities as they relate to Windows forms. New controls such as MaskedTextBox, WebBrowser, ToolStrip, and MenuStrip allow for visually pleasing and full-featured applications to be built more easily. New containers such as FlowLayoutPanel, TableLayoutPanel, and SplitPanel allow you to build a user interface that gracefully handles resizing. These capabilities will allow you to quickly build more sophisticated and professional looking applications with less code and less work.

Chapter 4: Enhancements to Web Application Development

This chapter looks at ASP.NET 2.0 and Visual Basic 2005 enhancements and how they apply to building Web applications. Master pages and themes allow a standard look and feel for a Web application to easily be established. The addition of security controls and membership allow application authentication and authorization to be addressed with almost no code.

Chapter 5: Enhancements to Mobile Application Development

This chapter covers building mobile applications with Visual Basic 2005 and the .NET Compact Framework. Most of what was covered in previous chapters still applies to building mobile applications that will run on Pocket PC and Smartphone devices. The differences between the .NET Framework and the .NET Compact Framework, as well as differences between Pocket PC and Smartphone, will be reviewed.

Chapter 6: Data Management with ADO.NET

The last chapter covers the enhanced capabilities of ADO .NET 2.0. These capabilities allow easier database access and more flexibility for accessing XML or database data. The ability to present data in a master-detail format will be explored, as well as building and using a user interface to allow subsets of data to be retrieved from the database. The benefits of using parameterized queries are also covered.

Appendix A: ClickOnce Deployment

The appendix covers a new feature of Visual Studio 2005 called ClickOnce deployment. The goal of ClickOnce is to make it as easy to install and update desktop applications as it is to install and update Web applications.

Key Features

The following pedagogical elements lend structure and organization to the text:

- Learning objectives are identified at the beginning of each chapter, so the reader is aware of what to expect.
- Examples are illustrated with numerous screen shots to allow the reader to follow along with ease.

- Chapter summaries identify the key points in a descriptive, bulleted list format. The summaries equip the reader with a mechanism to review the chapter's key concepts quickly.
- Key terms are highlighted in boldface type to quickly identify the new terminology presented in each chapter.

Acknowledgements

The author would like to recognize the contributions of the following individuals who assisted in improving the quality of the manuscript by serving as reviewers: Cliff Brozo, Monroe College, and Bill Sypawka, Pitt Community College.

There were many people at Thomson Course Technology who made an important contribution to this book. Tricia Boyle, Mac Mendelsohn, Jill Klaffky, and Drew Strawbridge all played a valuable role in this project.

Read This Before You Begin

In order to to release this book to coincide with the launch of Visual Studio 2005 in November 2005, it was written using Visual Studio 2005 Professional Beta 2. Because some topics covered may have changed in the final product, I will attempt to list any updates on my Web site, *http://www.martinschray.com.*

Visual Studio 2005 adds several additional editions to those that came with Visual Studio .NET 2003. We will quickly explore the Visual Studio 2005 editions and how they differ, but ultimately the one you select will vary based on your needs and what you are trying to accomplish.

This text assumes usage of Visual Studio 2005 Professional Edition and Visual Basic 2005. Why are Visual Studio 2005 and Visual Basic 2005 listed together? In addition to Visual Basic 2005, Visual Studio 2005 includes a number of programming languages such as C# and J#.

If you are using or planning to use a different version of Visual Studio 2005, all topics that are covered in this text will still apply with a few notable exceptions. Visual Basic 2005 Express Edition will not support mobile applications development, ClickOnce deployment, the Object Designer and the Object Test Workbench. Additionally, if you are using Visual Basic 2005 Express Edition and want to do Web development you will need to install Visual Web Developer 2005 Express Edition. The following table is provided to allow quick comparisons between versions.

Visual Studio 2005 Version	Visual Basic 2005	Win forms Applications	Web Applications	Mobile Applications	Click Once	Object Designer/ Test Workbench
Visual Basic 2005 Express Edition	Yes	Yes	Requires Visual Web Developer 2005 Express Edition	No	No	No
Visual Studio Standard Edition	Yes	Yes	Yes	Yes	Yes	Yes

(continued)

Visual Studio 2005 Version	Visual Basic 2005	Win forms Applica-tions	Web Applica-tions	Mobile Applica-tions	Click Once	Object Designer/ Test Workbench
Visual Studio Professional Edition	Yes	Yes	Yes	Yes	Yes	Yes
Visual Studio Tools for Office	Yes	Yes	Yes	No	No	Yes
Visual Studio Team System	Yes	Yes	Yes	Yes	Yes	Yes

Using Your Own Computer

You will need one of the versions of Visual Studio 2005 that are listed in the table. In addition, to develop the programs in this book, you will need the following:

- Processor: 600 MHz Pentium II-class processor (minimum)
  - 1 GHz Pentium III-class processor (recommended)
- Operating System: Windows 2000 or Windows XP
- Software: Visual Basic 2005 Professional Edition or Visual Basic 2005 Express Edition
- Memory: 192 MB RAM (minimum)
  - 256 MB RAM (recommended)
- Hard Disk Space: 500 MB of available space on system drive
  - 1.5 GB available space on installation drive
  - 1.9 GB additional space for MSDN library documentation
- Drive: CD-ROM or DVD-ROM drive
- Display: Super VGA or higher resolution display with 256 colors
- Mouse or compatible pointing device

CHAPTER

1

ENHANCEMENTS TO VISUAL STUDIO 2005

In this chapter you will:

- Learn about the new Class Designer, Object Test Bench, and refactoring support in Visual Studio 2005
- Understand the use of the Project Designer's Settings pane to store application and user configuration and settings information
- Leverage the new debugger DataTips and visualizations to get more useful debug information about your application
- Apply recommendations from the Exception Assistant dialog box to correct runtime problems with your application
- Learn to utilize Edit and Continue
- Use code snippets to easily complete common programming tasks
- Apply the recommendations from the Error Correction dialog box to correct compile errors

Visual Studio 2005 has a large number of new features that are designed to make building Visual Basic 2005 applications much easier. This chapter explores the new features of Visual Studio 2005 in the form of new and enhanced designers, as well as other Visual Studio User Interface enhancements that allow you to create, test, and revise your applications more quickly.

Some changes are pretty noticeable; for example, when you create a new Windows Forms application there are a number of new classes that are generated for you. The biggest new additions are the new designers. Designers allow you to visually interact with Visual Studio 2005 to create your application.

Visual Studio 2005 introduces the Class Designer and the Object Test Bench. The Class Designer allows you to create classes by visually supplying the properties, methods, and other aspects of a class without writing code. The Object Test Bench is a new designer that you use in conjunction with the Class Designer to test your new classes. The Project Designer has a number of new capabilities, but its new support for creating, modifying, and deleting application and user settings will probably be of the most interest to developers.

Finally, Visual Studio 2005 tries to provide helpful information when you need it. The debugger adds DataTips and visualizations that make it much easier to see your data in the debugger, and the Error Correction dialog box provides suggested fixes to common compile errors. You will cover new features such as the code snippets library, the ability to provide XML documentation, and Edit and Continue.

Class Designer

There may be times when a program's code is spread throughout a numbers of files, but you really want to see all the different pieces graphically. The **Class Designer** allows you to see your classes visually by providing a diagram of your classes. After reviewing the capabilities of the Class Designer, you will explore a short example to gain an understanding of how to use the Class Designer.

The Class Designer displays a class's methods, properties, fields, events, and other members in a compact graphical format, as shown in Figure 1-1. The class diagram depicted in Figure 1-1 shows the standard generated classes that are part of a Visual Basic Windows application.

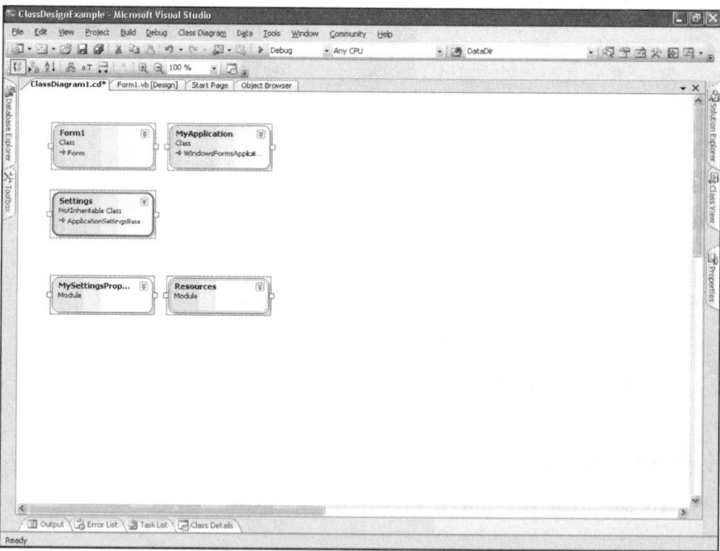

Figure 1-1 The Class Designer

The Class Designer allows you to graphically define, view, modify, rename, and delete the following class members:

- Methods
- Properties
- Fields
- Events
- Constructors
- Destructors
- Constants

Additionally, the Class Designer allows you to drag and drop items from the Toolbox to add the following types to the class diagram:

- Class
- Enum
- Interface
- Abstract Class
- Structure
- Delegate
- Module
- Inheritance relationship
- Association
- Comment

Figure 1-2 shows the Class Designer toolbox. Just as you would drag controls such as buttons and labels onto a form, the Class Designer toolbox allows types such as classes, structures, and modules to be dragged onto the Class Designer.

The best way to understand the capabilities of the Class Designer is to walk through an example. In the following section, a simple calculator application will be built, starting with a standard Visual Basic 2005 Windows application and using the Class Designer to add additional functionality.

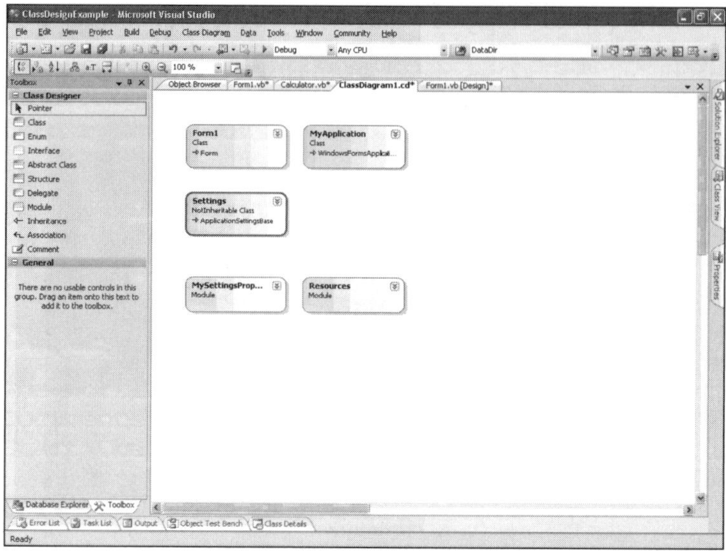

Figure 1-2 Class Designer Toolbox

Class Designer Example: Building a Calculator

The first step in this example is to create a new Visual Basic 2005 Windows application.

1. On the VS 2005 menu bar click **File**, then click **New**, then click **Project** to open the dialog box shown in Figure 1-3.

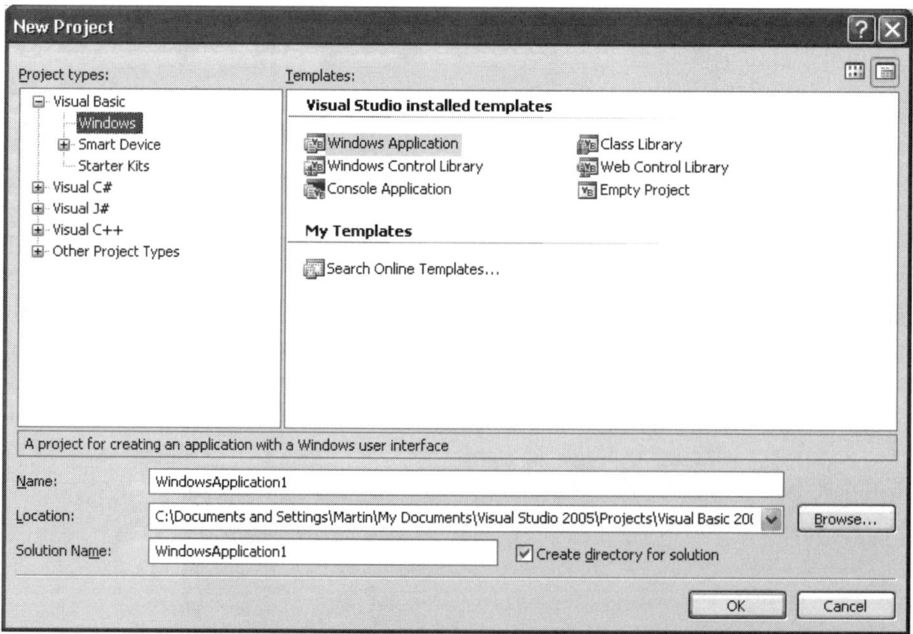

Figure 1-3 New Project dialog box

2. Click **Windows Application** to create the new application, then press **OK**.
3. The Class Designer for your application can be accessed through the Solution Explorer (to open the Solution Explorer use **Ctrl+Alt+L**, or on the VS 2005 menu bar click **View**, then click **Solution Explorer**).
4. Once the Solution Explorer is visible, right-click the **project** and click **View Class Diagram**, as shown in Figure 1-4. This causes a class diagram to be built for your current project.

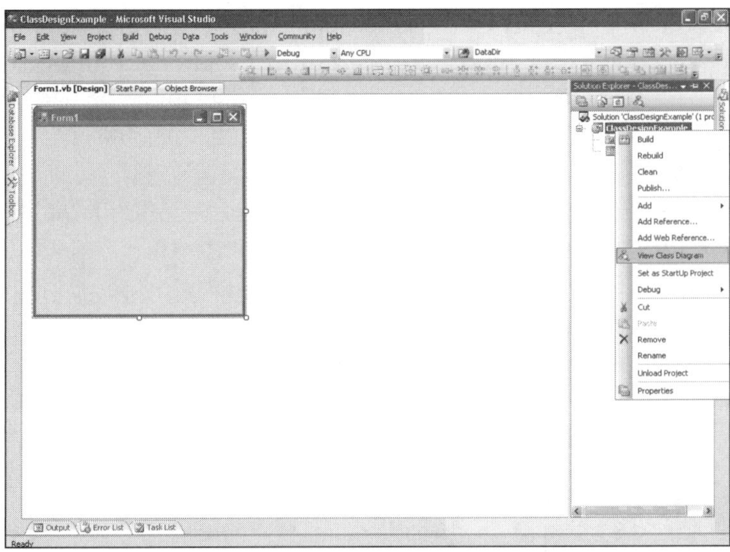

Figure 1-4 Opening the Class Designer

Figure 1-1 showed the class diagram that is built for a standard Windows Forms project. Visual Studio .NET 2003 generated a single class named Form1.vb for a Windows Forms application. Visual Studio 2005 takes a few extra steps compared to Visual Studio 2003. In addition to the default form (Form1) that is generated, there are a number of other classes and modules that are generated. The classes and modules that Visual Studio 2005 generates are listed in Table 1-1.

Table 1-1 Visual Basic 2005 generated project code

Class/Module Name	Purpose
Form1	The main form of the application
MyApplication	This is where the generated code that defines how the user interface will look is placed; additionally, it includes the application's main function.
Settings	This class is used by My.Settings.Properties.

Table 1-1 Visual Basic 2005 generated project code (continued)

Class/Module Name	Purpose
MySettingProperties	This module uses the Settings class to provide easy access to any application settings.
Resources	This module provides easy access to any text or image resources that might have been stored in assemblies.

Adding Functionality

Next, you'll build on the functionality of the basic application that is currently in the Class Designer. The goal is to build a four-function calculator that supports addition, subtraction, multiplication, and division. After giving it some careful consideration, the decision is made to put the code to support the four-function calculator into its own class.

1. The first step is to make sure the Class Designer is open. On the VS 2005 menu bar click **View**, then **Solution Explorer**. Once the Solution Explorer is visible, right-click the **project** and click **View Class Diagram**.
2. Next, create the class that will have the calculator functionality. In the Class Designer, click **Ctrl+Alt+X** to open the Toolbox. Or, click **View**, then **Toolbox** on the VS 2005 menu bar.
3. Click the item labeled **Class** in the Toolbox, then drag and drop it onto the Class Designer. The New Class dialog box opens, as shown in Figure 1-5.

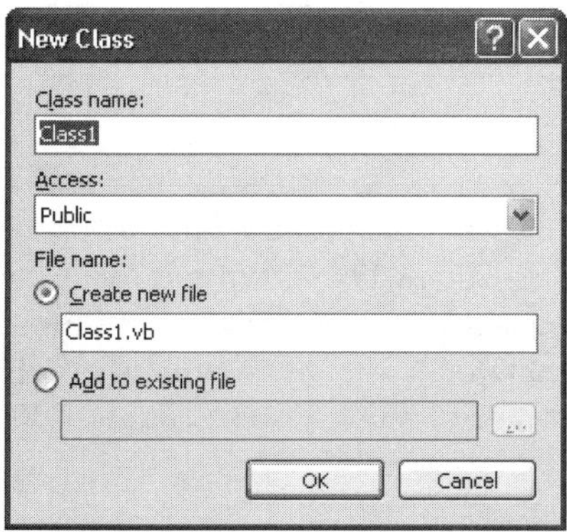

Figure 1-5 New Class dialog box

4. The class name should be changed to something meaningful such as Calculator. Click **OK** and the new class appears in the Class Designer, as depicted in Figure 1-6.
5. Right-click the new **Calculator** class and click **Class Details** on the context menu (Figure 1-7), and the Class Details window opens (Figure 1-6). The Class Details window can be used to add, edit, and modify methods, properties, fields, and events.

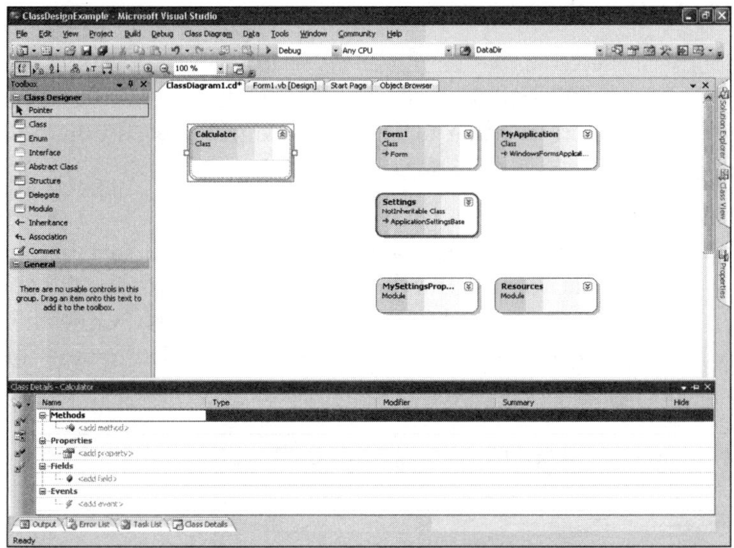

Figure 1-6 Class Designer with class details

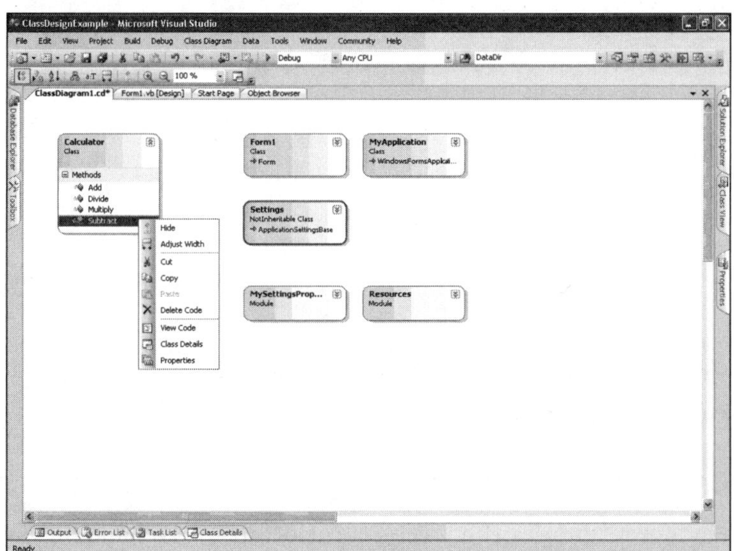

Figure 1-7 Class context menu choices

Using the Class Details window methods for add, subtract, multiply, and divide for the Calculator class could easily be added.

Creating Inheritance Relationships

An additional capability of the Class Designer is to allow inheritance relationships between objects to be specified. You will expand on the simple calculator example to see how the Class Designer can be used to create inheritance relationships between objects.

Although Object Oriented Programming takes practice and discipline to get right, using the Class Designer to build inheritance relationships is quite easy. The Class Designer has the capability to allow inheritance relationships between objects to be specified with a few mouse clicks (e.g., SuperCalculator is inherited from Calculator). While in the Class Designer, simply go to the Toolbox and drag and drop a new class. Name the new class SuperCalculator using the technique described above. Your new class appears in the Class Designer as shown in Figure 1-8.

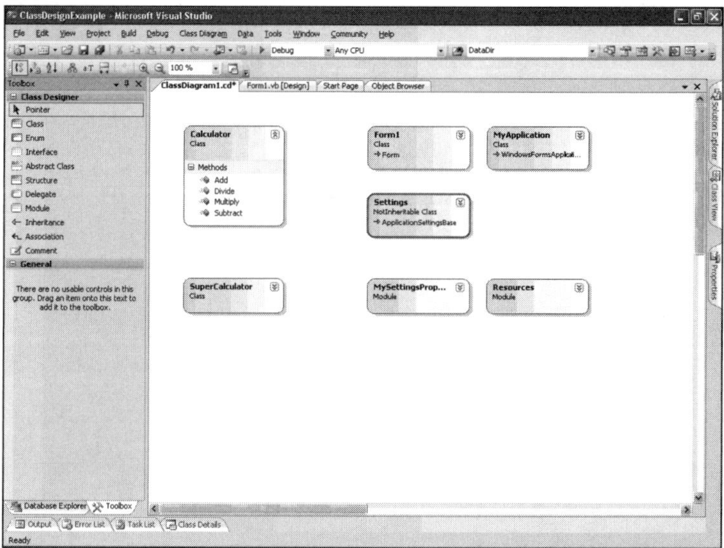

Figure 1-8 Setting up SuperCalculator to inherit from Calculator

Establishing an Inheritance Relationship

To establish an inheritance relationship between Calculator (base class) and SuperCalculator (subclass), simply follow these three steps.

1. Click the **Inheritance** item in the Toolbox.
2. Click the subclass **(SuperCalculator)** and then click the base class **(Calculator)**. Figure 1-9 shows the result after this step has been completed. Note that SuperCalculator now has an arrow connected to Calculator to indicate it is inherited from Calculator.

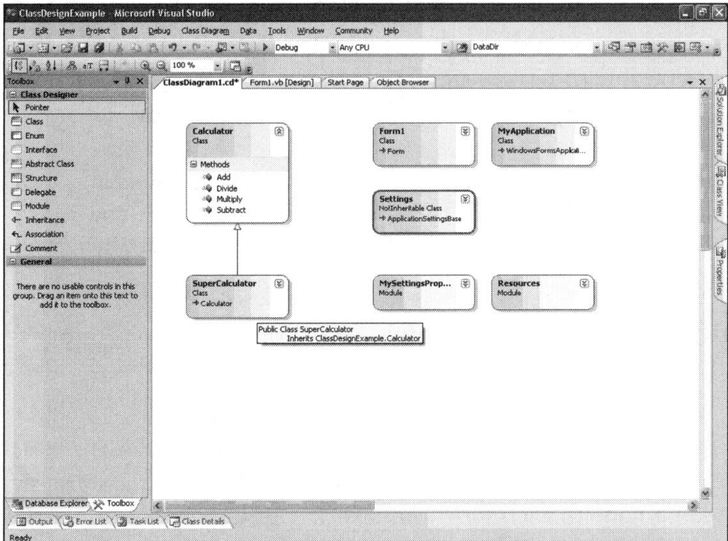

Figure 1-9 SuperCalculator is inherited from Calculator

3. Additionally, if you place the mouse pointer over SuperCalculator, a floating window indicates that it inherits from Calculator, and there is a small arrow in the diagram for SuperCalculator indicating its parent is Calculator.

Class Designer vs. Code Editor

The Class Designer and your code are synchronized as changes are made in either the Class Designer or the Code Editor. For example, if you add a method to a class using the Code Editor, the method automatically appears in the Class Designer as well. Figure 1-9 depicts the Calculator class after the Add, Divide, Multiply, and Subtract methods have been added. Accessing the code for a method from the Class Designer is pretty straightforward.

1. Select and right-click the method for which you would like to view source code.
2. On the context-menu click **View Code**, as depicted back in Figure 1-7. The View Code menu choice takes you to the selected method's code in the Code Editor.

The Class Designer can be used to graphically add or remove arguments, add or remove methods, and leverage other basic class-editing capabilities. The Class Designer is a very rich and full-featured tool for graphically building the classes in your application. The Class Designer is supposed to be used in conjunction with the Object Test Bench to test the classes that you build with the Class Designer.

Object Test Bench

Wouldn't it be great to be able to write a simple function and test it without having to write most of the application? If so, then the Object Test Bench is for you.

If the thought of testing never crosses your mind, then here is something new to consider. It is always a good idea to test even the simplest code, and using the Object Test Bench makes it easy. As I like to say: Test early, test often, and test always.

The **Object Test Bench** is meant to be a simple design time test tool. Rather then having to compile, build, and execute your application to test the behavior of new code at runtime, the Object Test Bench allows you to test your classes from the Class Designer.

A good example of the type of testing the Object Test Bench is meant for is a basic test of the Calculator class. After defining the Add, Subtract, Multiply, and Divide functions using the Class Designer and then adding code to each function to carry out the required operation, it would be good to test the methods to see if they actually work properly. You could go through the effort of building your calculator user interface (textboxes, buttons, and such), but that seems like a lot of work just to see if the Add method works correctly. Instead, the Object Test Bench makes testing basic object methods much easier, as shown in the following steps.

1. In the Class Designer, right-click the **Calculator** class to open its context-menu. Select **Create Instance**, and then click **Calculator**, as shown in Figure 1-10. This causes the Create Instance dialog box to open.
2. Click **OK** in the Create Instance dialog box to open the Object Test Bench with an instance of the Calculator class ready to be tested.
3. Right-click the **Calculator1** object in the Object Test Bench. A context-menu opens and allows you to call the various methods on the Calculator object, as shown in Figure 1-11.

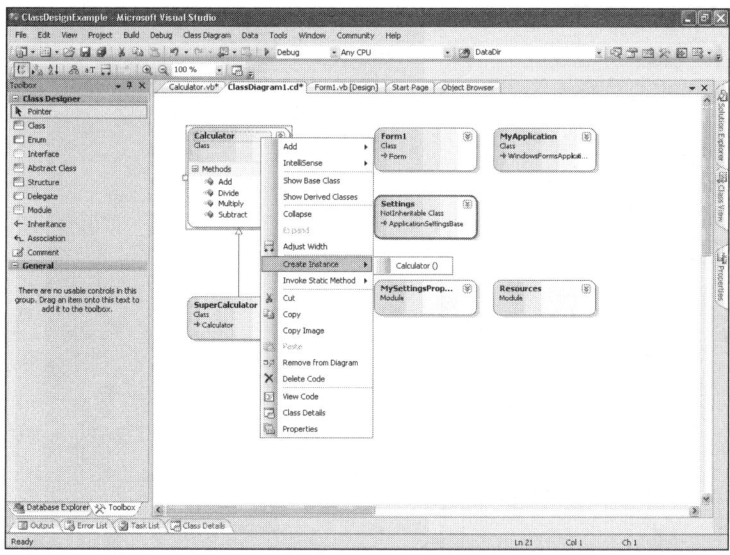

Figure 1-10 Creating an instance of the Calculator class for the Object Test Bench

4. Click **Add (Integer, Integer)** to open a dialog box that prompts for the input values for the invoked method. Figure 1-12 shows this dialog box after the value of 10 has been entered for both Integer arguments of the Add method. Figure 1-13 shows the Method Call Result dialog box. Obviously adding 10 and 10 is not equal to 0, so there is a bug in the code. A quick inspection of the code reveals the programmer forgot to provide the code for the Add method.

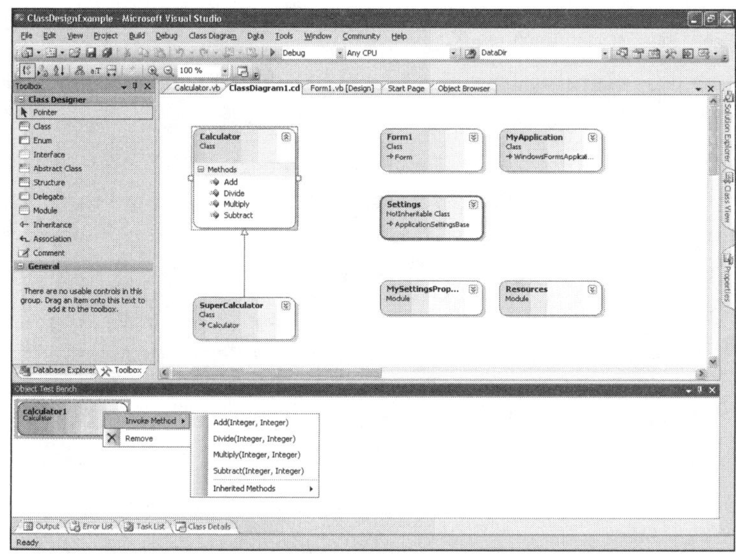

Figure 1-11 Selecting the method to test

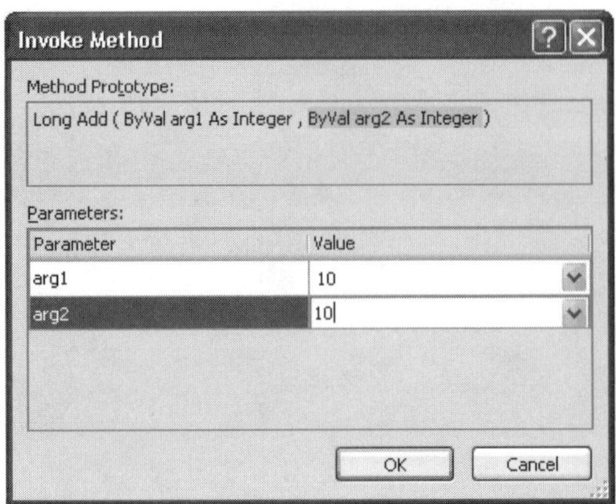

Figure 1-12 Providing the arguments to invoke the method

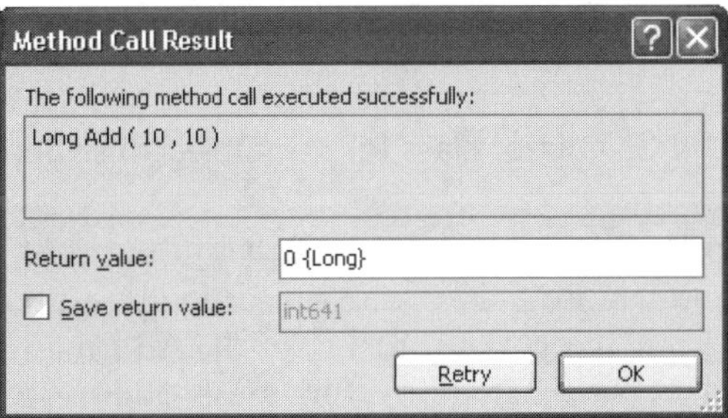

Figure 1-13 Method Call Result dialog box showing incorrect results

Figure 1-13 shows there is an option to save the method call result. The purpose of saving the result from a method call would be to use the result from the method call for another test. Figure 1-14 shows that the result from the Add method has been saved and is now being used to invoke another method.

The Object Test Bench also allows shared functions to be easily tested. For example, if a shared method named "Square" was added to the Calculator class, it could easily be tested by right-clicking the Calculator class, selecting Invoke Static Method, then clicking the Square method to open the Object Test Bench. Then you can use the procedures outlined previously to test the Square method.

The Object Test Bench can be used to test simple functions at design time rather than having to write and compile code to test functionality at runtime.

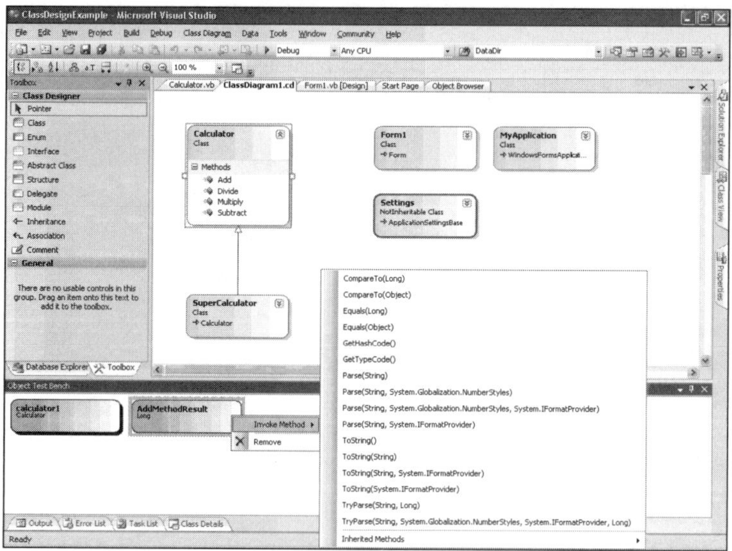

Figure 1-14 Invoke a method on a saved result

Project Designer

It would be helpful if all the major settings and configuration information for an entire application was in one single location. The **Project Designer** has been upgraded to use a tab pane metaphor, similar to the tabs in a notebook, as shown in Figure 1-15, to keep all application settings and configuration information in one place. The existing capabilities of the Project Designer have been enhanced, and a number of new capabilities have been added as well.

The functionality in the Application, Compile, Debug, and References panes have largely been available since Visual Studio .NET 2003, although there are some new options that have been added. The Settings, Resources, Signing, Security, and Publish panes are all new capabilities. The Signing, Security, and Publish panes all relate to ClickOnce deployment, which will be covered in Appendix A. The Resources pane provides capabilities for internationalization of applications. Internationalization of application is a very complex topic that can easily fill another text, and it is not addressed here.

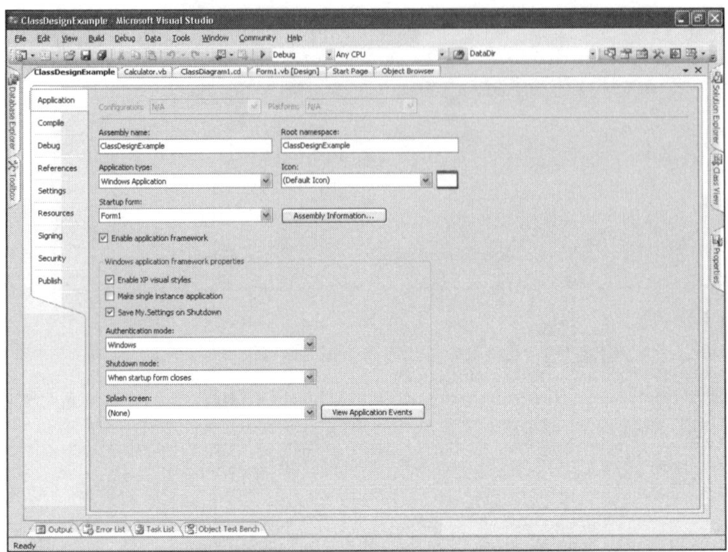

Figure 1-15 The Project Designer

Most applications have settings that act as key application configuration information. Settings are of great importance to developers, and the capabilities of the Settings pane is of immediate use to most developers, so it is covered here in some detail. Basic information on all the Project Designer panes can be found in Table 1-2.

Table 1-2 Project Designer panes

Project Designer pane	Function
Application	Visual Studio .NET 2003 had a General dialog box in the Project Designer under Common Properties in the menu bar. This contained information about a project namespace, assembly name, icon, and other application properties. The Visual Studio 2005 Project Designer Application pane takes the General setting from Visual Studio .NET 2003 and adds a number of new ones such as: • Access to application events • The ability to allow only a single copy of an application to run; when the Make single instance application check box is checked, only one copy of the application can be running at a time. • Whether to use XP Visual Styles by default • The ability to supply a startup or splash screen when an application starts • Some additional application settings such as authentication type (windows or application defined)

Table 1-2 Project Designer panes (continued)

Project Designer pane	Function
Compile	Visual Studio .NET 2003 had a Build Events dialog box in the Project Designer that could be found in the Build and Common Properties menu under Configuration Properties. The Visual Studio 2005 Project Designer Compile pane takes the General setting and Build Events from Visual Studio .NET 2003 and combines them into the Compile pane.
Debug	Visual Studio .NET 2003 had a Debugging dialog box in the Project Designer under Configuration Properties on the menu bar. The Visual Studio 2005 Project Designer Debug pane takes the Debugging settings from Visual Studio .NET 2003 and places them into the Compile pane.
References	Visual Studio .NET 2003 had a Reference Paths dialog box and an Imports dialog box in the Project Designer found under Common Properties on the menu bar. The Visual Studio 2005 Project Designer Reference pane combines the settings from Reference Paths and Imports.
Settings	This pane allows both application and user-level settings to be created and maintained for an application. The Settings pane is basically a setting editor that allows settings to be added, deleted, or edited.
Resources	This pane is typically used to extract application resources such as strings and graphs for applications that must support multiple languages or cultures. The resources pane is basically an editor that allows resources to be added, deleted, or edited.
Signing	This pane is used to specify digital certificates used to sign applications to ensure application authenticity and identify the developer of the application.
Security	This pane is used to indicate what level of access to system resources (file, printers, clipboard) this application has. The Security pane is meant to be used in conjunction with the Publish pane because it only allows security settings for ClickOnce deployment to be specified.
Publish	This pane is used to configure ClickOnce deployment settings for applications that use ClickOnce deployment.

If you are using Visual Studio 2005 Team Suite there will be a tab for Code Analysis. Code Analysis helps ensure the quality and consistency of the code you develop.

Settings Pane

Almost every application has the need for custom configuration or setting information. Hard coding this information directly in the application is typically not a good solution, because the information can vary for each user of the application and would require the application to be recompiled for each change.

Application settings typically fall into one of two broad categories. The first category of settings is application settings such as database names, file locations, and database connection strings. The second category of settings is application user settings. Some examples of user settings data might be a user id, a directory to be used to store a user's application data, how often to update application data, or the user's zip code.

Historically, the approach used for storing settings data has been to store it in a text file. More recently many developers have begun to prefer storing data in **Extensible Markup Language (XML)** files. XML is a mechanism for defining what data should be in a file as well as the actual data for the file. The following example provides a small section of an XML file that stores a user's zip code and how often the user would like the application to be updated. The contents of this XML example were generated by the Settings pane.

```
<ClassDesignerExample.Settings>
    <setting name="Zipcode" serializeAs="String">
        <value>60005</value>
    </setting>
    <setting name="UpdateInterval" serializeAs="String">
         <value>10</value>
    </setting>
</ClassDesignerExample.Settings>
```

The Settings pane allows application and user settings to be quickly and easily defined and stored in an XML file created by the Settings pane. Figure 1-16 shows the Settings pane being used to create settings for the user's Zipcode and UpdateInterval settings.

In most cases it is equally important to be able to easily read and update setting data programmatically. In conjunction with the Settings pane, there are two generated classes that are part of the project; these classes are named Settings and MySettingsProperties. These two classes work in harmony with a new programming approach called My, which is a part of Visual Basic 2005. Chapter 2 will cover My in some level of detail. The following example is covered in detail in Chapter 2, but is provided here to show the ease with which settings can be retrieved, updated, and saved. The following Zipcode and UpdateInterval settings were created in the Settings pane in Figure 1-16.

```
' get the Zipcode setting
Dim zipCode As Integer = My.Settings.Zipcode

' get the UpdateInterval setting
Dim updateInterval As Integer =_
My.Settings.UpdateInterval
```

1

```
' save 60604 as the new zipcode
My.Settings.Zipcode = 60604

' save the settings back to the app.config file
My.Settings.Save()
```

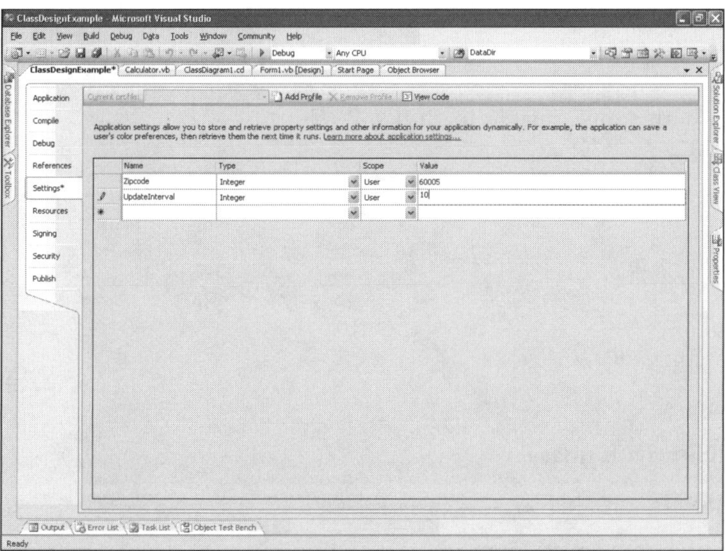

Figure 1-16 Example of Project Designer's Settings pane

REFACTORING

Changing the order of arguments passed to a method and then finding out the method was used in a number of locations in a program can potentially be a problem. You are then faced with a seemingly endless list of compile errors. If you have had this experience, you might have thought Visual Studio .NET 2003 should really make this much easier. Refactoring support in Visual Basic 2005 is designed to address this problem.

Refactoring is the process of making changes to existing code to make it more readable, reusable, and better structured. Refactoring can be as simple as renaming classes, methods, variables, and arguments. Refactoring can also involve more-complicated changes such as extracting blocks of code into separate methods, reordering or renaming parameters, promoting a local variable into instance variable, and a number of other similar operations. Historically, developers have performed these types of refactoring operations manually without any support from Visual Studio .NET 2003.

Refactoring support is built into C# 2005, but is not built directly into Visual Basic 2005. The good news is that Microsoft will be providing refactoring support for Visual Basic 2005 via a free download. The following types of refactoring will be supported in Visual Basic 2005:

- Reorder parameters
- Extract method
- Extract property
- Create overload
- Surrounds with (not available in BETA 2 release)
- Encapsulate field
- Reverse conditional
- Simplify expression
- Introduce local
- Introduce constant
- Inline temp
- Replace temp with query
- Split temporary variable
- Move initialization to declaration
- Split initialization from declaration
- Move declaration near reference

Debugger DataTips and Visualization

Debugging an application is often challenging. Attempting to look at the contents of a somewhat complex class such as ArrayList using a debugger can be daunting. The Visual Studio 2005 Debugger has been enhanced with **DataTips** and **visualizations**. DataTips and visualizations have the goal of making it much easier to view complex data while using the debugger. DataTips allow you to see the critical data for complex objects, such as being able to easily view the actual values stored in an ArrayList. Visualizations can be thought of as viewers that know how to format data so that it can easily be viewed. For example, there is a visualization that knows how to format a string of HTML into a format easy to read by humans.

Accessing debugger DataTips and visualizations is as simple as holding the mouse pointer stationary (hovering) over a variable while using the debugger. Figure 1-17 shows the DataTip for a string variable. By selecting the down arrow in the DataTips, you can select the proper visualizer for your string data. By default there are visualizers for text, XML, and

HTML data. By selecting one of these visualizers the data is displayed in a dialog box to allow closer inspection of the data, as shown in Figure 1-18. One of the benefits of the visualizers is that they allow character wrap and scrolling so it is easy to look at long strings.

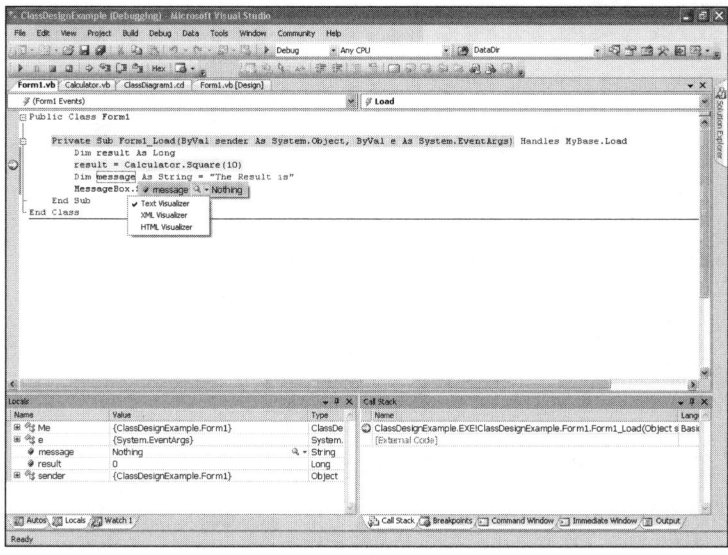

Figure 1-17 DataTips for a string object

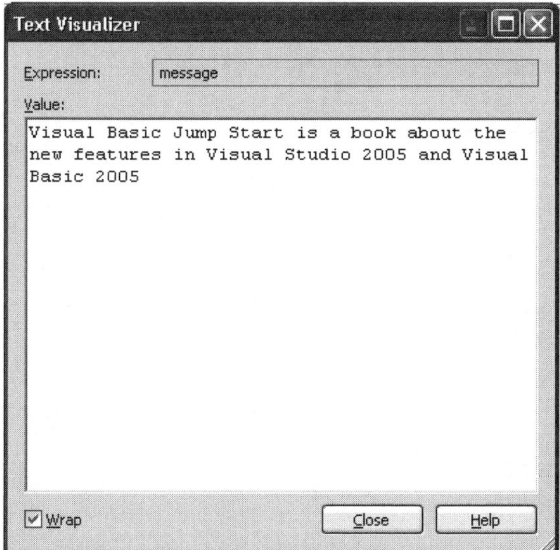

Figure 1-18 Text visualizer

Figure 1-19 shows the DataTips for an ArrayList variable. The DataTips makes it quite easy to see the number of elements in the ArrayList as well as the value for each of the elements. If the elements contained more large and complex strings or strings that were XML or HTML, the visualizers could be used to more easily view the contained data.

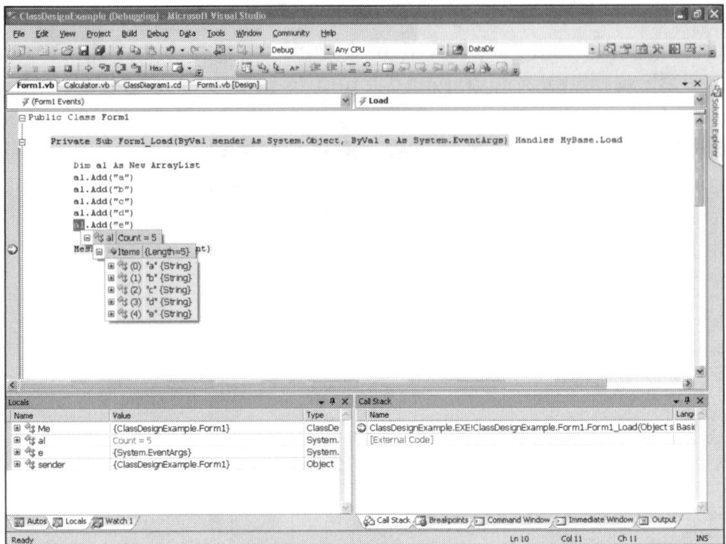

Figure 1-19 DataTips for ArrayList

In addition to the DataTips for built-in classes such as String and ArrayList, the debugger can generate DataTips for classes that you have designed. Figure 1-20 shows the DataTips for a user-defined type named Student. Student has properties for Age, Birthday, GPA, and Name, and the DataTips does a pretty good job of showing these properties.

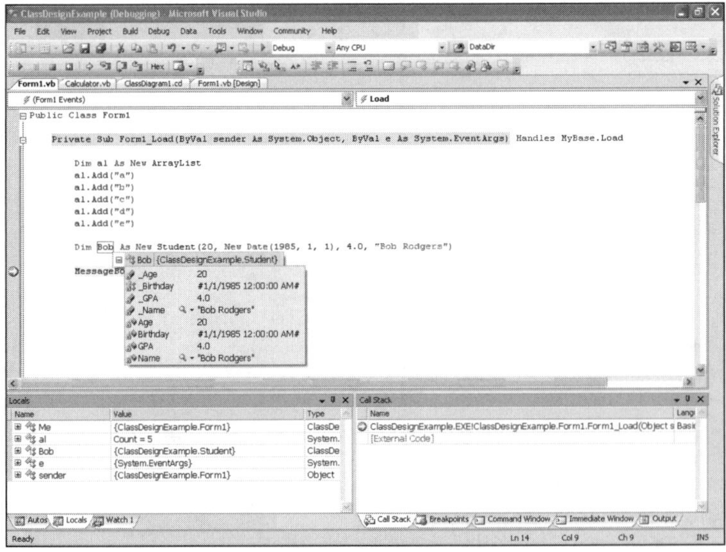

Figure 1-20 DataTips for a user-defined class

EDIT AND CONTINUE

Edit and Continue was actually a feature that was in Visual Basic 6.0, but didn't find its way into Visual Studio .NET 2002 or Visual Studio .NET 2003. The good news is that it is back in Visual Studio 2005. **Edit and Continue** allows you to be more productive because source changes can be made during a debugging session without having to exit the debugger, make changes, recompile, and restart the debugger.

There may be times you see an obvious bug in your code when using a debugger. For example, Figure 1-21 shows three lines of code. The first line declares a variable named Result, the second calls the Calculator Square method, and the third line displays the result. Stepping through the debugger you realize that the result returned from the Calculator Square method was never assigned to the result variable. Using Edit and Continue, you can simply edit the code while in the debugger and assign the returned value of the Calculator Square method call to the result variable and continue with your debugging session. Figure 1-22 shows the text "code changes were applied successfully" in the Visual Studio 2005 status bar, and a message box is displayed with the result of 100. With Edit and Continue you are able to correct this bug without exiting the debugger.

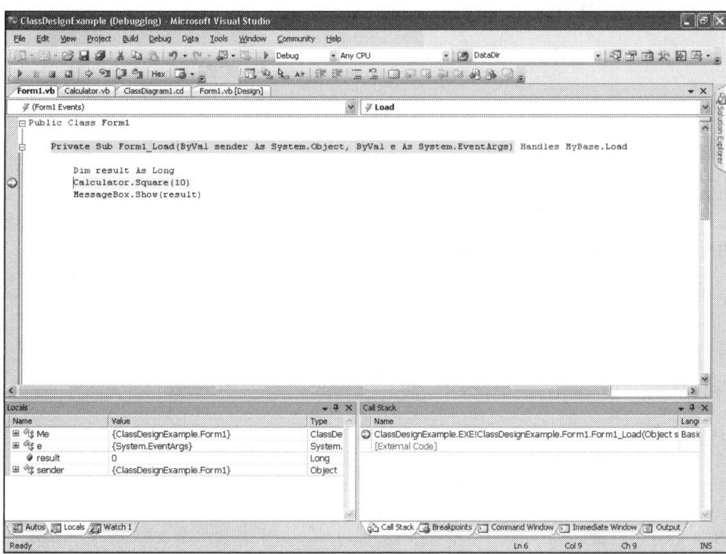

Figure 1-21 Edit and Continue

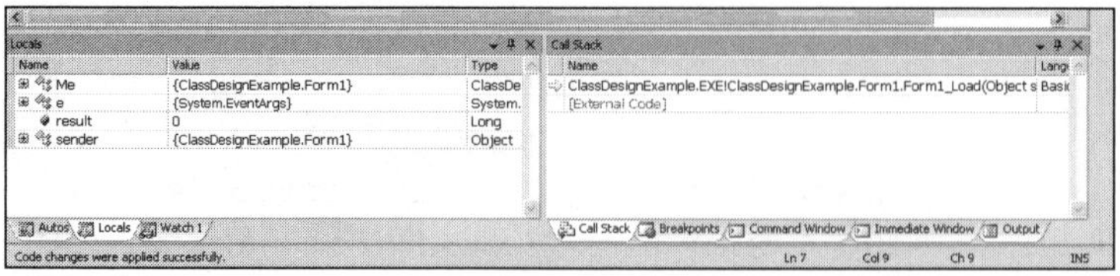

Figure 1-22 Making a code change while in the debugger

Code Snippets

Imagine if someone had taken the time to catalog and provide sample code for a large number of common programming tasks, such as creating a file, reading a file, and deleting a file. One of the challenges would be finding the block of code or snippet of code for the right task at the right time.

Code snippets provide a solution. They are organized in a huge library to allow you to easily find the one or ones best suited to complete a task at hand. The code snippets feature improves productivity by capturing commonly used programming tasks into a large, organized, and reusable collection.

Standard code snippets in Visual Basic 2005 are listed here:

- Application – Compiling, Resources, and Settings
- Collections
- Connectivity and Networking
- Data – Designer features and ADO.NET
- Data Types – Defined by Visual Basic
- File system – Processing Drives, Folder, and Files
- Globalization and Localization
- Math
- Security
- Visual Basic Language
- Web Services
- Windows Forms Applications
- Windows Operating System
- Working with Smart Devices
- XML

In addition, you can define your own code snippets and import code snippet libraries from others.

Accessing Code Snippets

Code snippets are selected by right-clicking the **Code Editor** and selecting **Insert Snippet** from the context-menu (Figure 1-23).

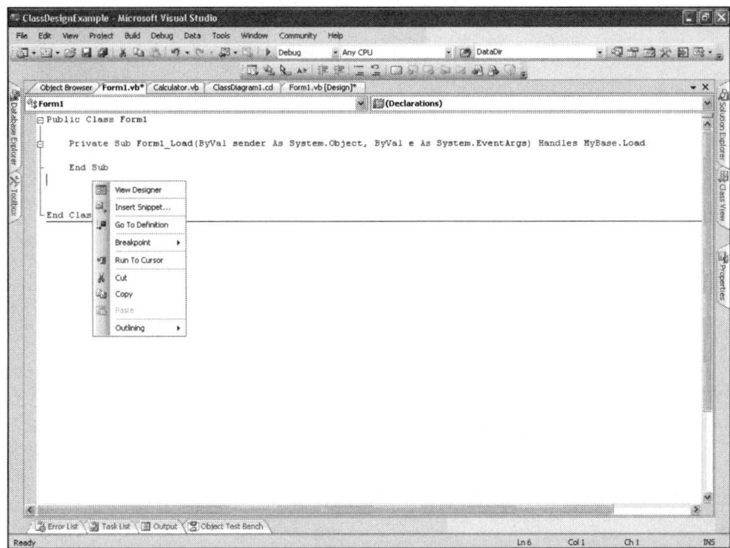

Figure 1-23 Getting to Insert Snippet

The text Insert Snippet appears with a set of categories to select from, as shown in Figure 1-24.

As an example, say your goal is to compare the contents of two files to see if they are equal. Sounds like a fairly challenging exercise. To do so, you need to open both files, read the contents, and compare the contents byte by byte to see if they are equal.

Figure 1-24 shows a folder in Code Snippets named File System. Selecting the File System folder expands it further into a specific set of tasks such as Compare files, Copy a directory, Open a file, and so on, as shown in Figure 1-25. Figure 1-26 shows how selecting Compare files inserts a new function that takes two file names as arguments and compares their contents. It returns "true" if the files match, or "false" if they don't.

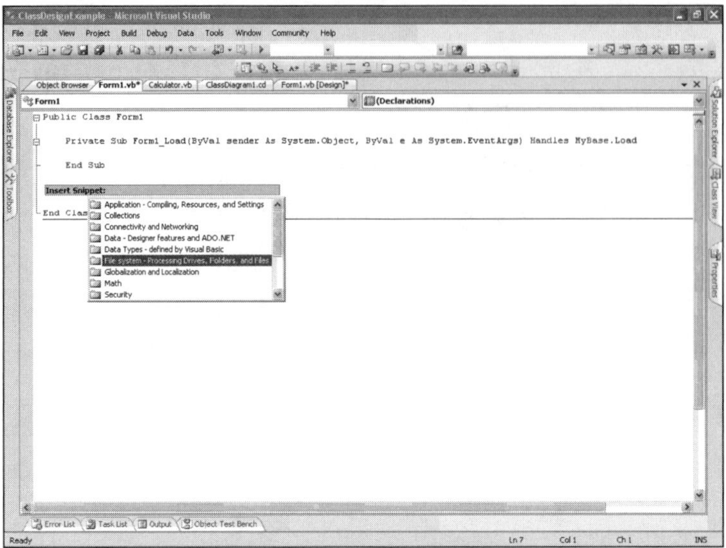

Figure 1-24 The categories of Insert Snippet

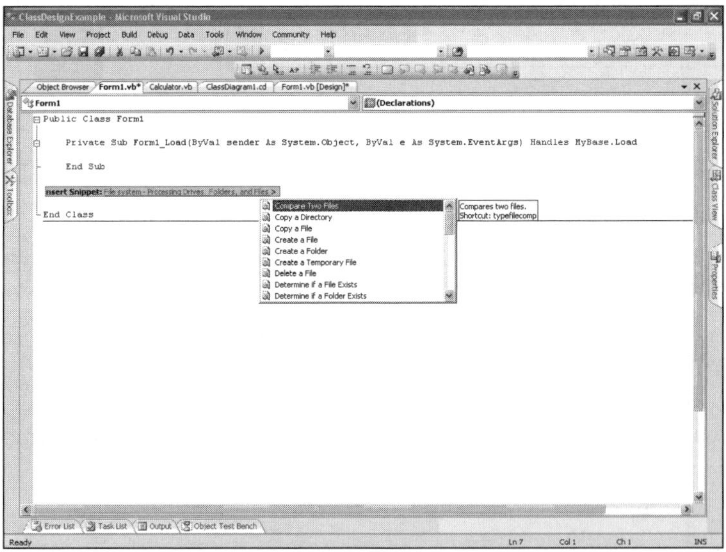

Figure 1-25 Insert a snippet to compare files

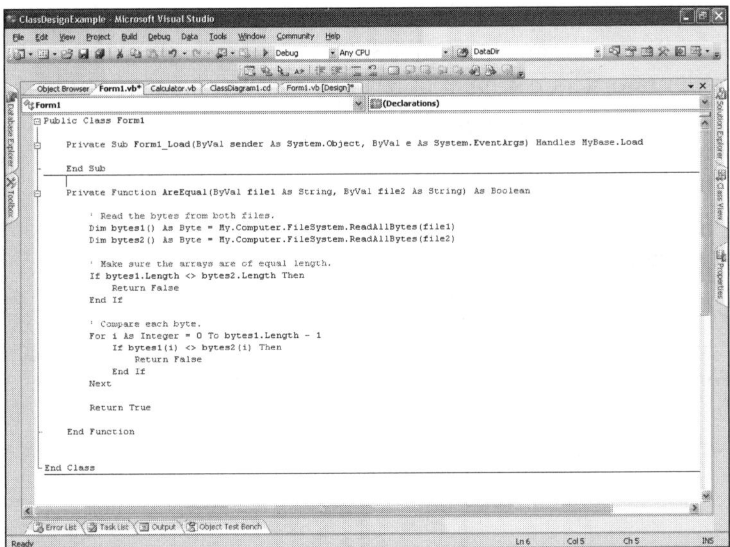

Figure 1-26 Inserted code from the code snippet library

Code Snippet Manager

Visual Studio 2005 also includes a **Code Snippet Manager** that allows code snippets to be added, removed, or imported, as Figure 1-27 illustrates. The Code Snippet Manager is opened by selecting the **VS 2005** menu, then choosing **Tools**, then **Code Snippet Manager**.

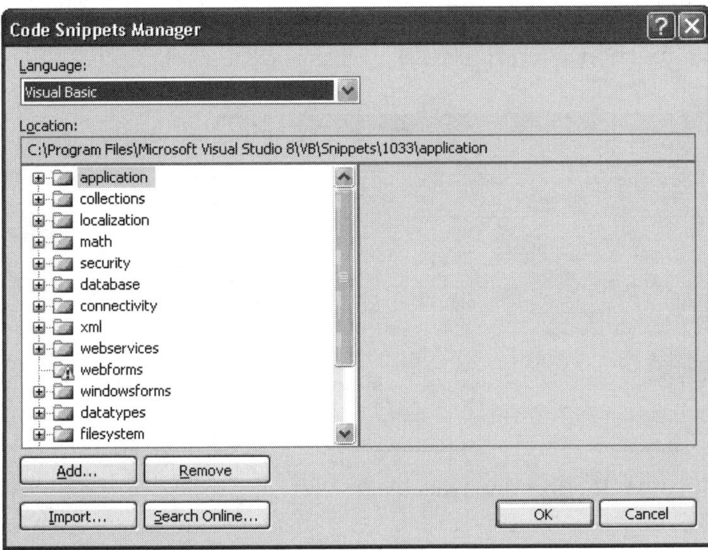

Figure 1-27 The Code Snippet Manager

There is a huge library of code snippets to draw from to complete everyday programming tasks. If you can't find what you need, the Code Snippet Manager allows you to define your own code snippets and import code snippet libraries from others. Visual Studio 2005 online help provides direction on how to develop, revise, and manage code snippets under the help topic "Creating and Using IntelliSense Code Snippets."

Miscellaneous Enhancements

There are a number of very useful additions to Visual Studio 2005 that are not as major as the Class Designer and Project Designer, but very useful nonetheless. This section covers XML documentation, starter kits, the Exception Assistant dialog box, the Error Correction dialog box, and the Track Changed lines feature in the Code Editor. These features are grouped together for convenience, but each is in its own right a powerful new capability in Visual Studio 2005.

XML Documentation

XML documentation has been a feature of the C# language since its inception. Visual Basic 2005 adds this capability. Why is it important? It allows the easy inclusion of documentation in a project. If there is a requirement that some level of documentation be included within your source files, you should probably consider XML documentation. XML documentation allows classes, methods, constants, fields, and properties to be documented easily.

To use XML documentation, simply place your cursor on the line directly above a method, field, constant, event, or property and type ''' (three comment characters). Visual Studio 2005 responds by generating the XML documentation appropriate for the method, field, constant, event, or property. For example, in the case of a method, it includes the function or subroutine name, any arguments, and if it is a function, a return type as well, as shown in Figure 1-28.

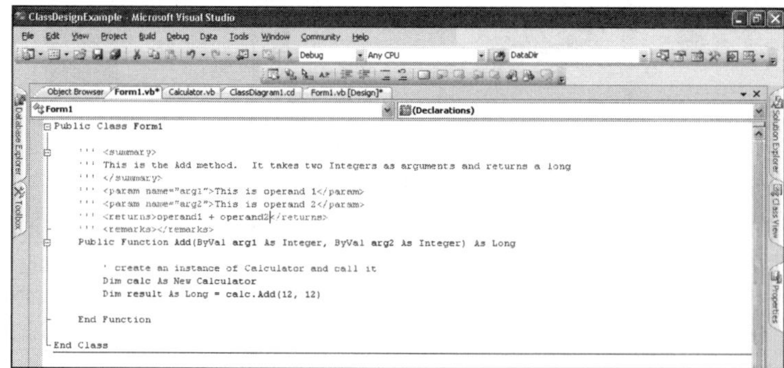

Figure 1-28 XML documentation now available in VB

Additionally, Visual Studio 2005 can generate HTML pages that extract the XML documentation and turn it into visually pleasing and easy-to-read HTML documents.

Starter Kits

Starter Kits are prebuilt application templates that allow you to build a new template application with a minimal amount of work. By default, Visual Studio 2005 comes with two Starter Kit projects, as Figure 1-29 illustrates. One of the Starter Kit applications allows you to track your movie collection, and a second Starter Kit allows you to build a screen saver. The Starter Kits are template applications that are not complete, but include step-by-step instructions for completing the applications.

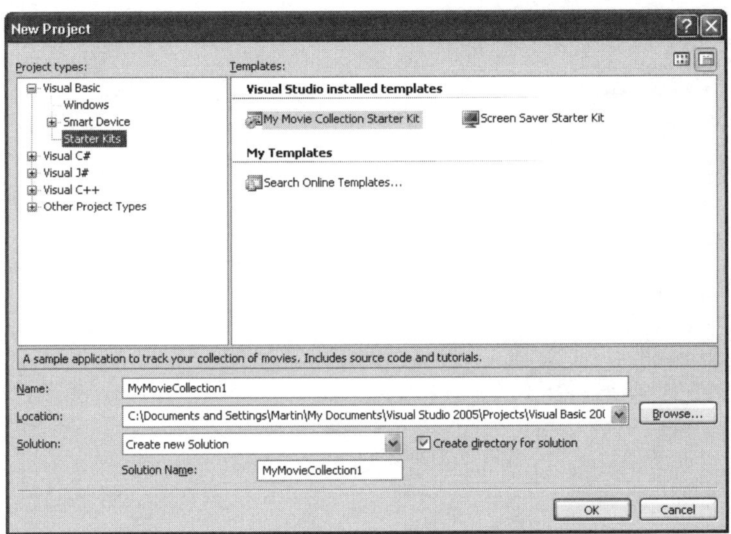

Figure 1-29 New Starter Kit project

Exception Assistant Dialog Box

The **Exception Assistant** provides more details on why an exception occurred in a running application and offers possible reasons for why the exception occurred. The Exception Assistant works in conjunction with the Debugger, so that when an exception is uncaught by application code, additional information and guidance on the potential causes of the exception can be offered to the developer. Figure 1-30 shows Visual Studio 2005 after an exception has occurred and the Exception Assistance dialog box is opened. Figure 1-31 shows the Troubleshooting tips that the Exception Assistant dialog box offers to resolve a FileNotFoundException. The tips that are provided in this case are pretty practical, suggesting that the developer verify that the file exists and that the path to the file is correct.

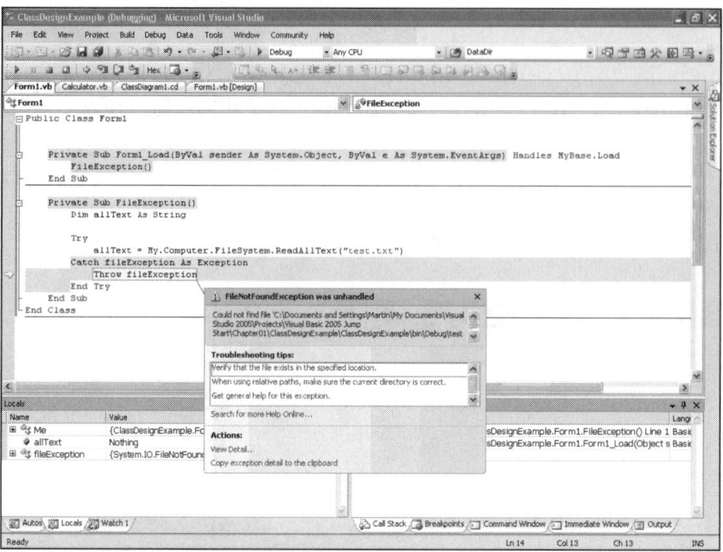

Figure 1-30 The Exception Assistant

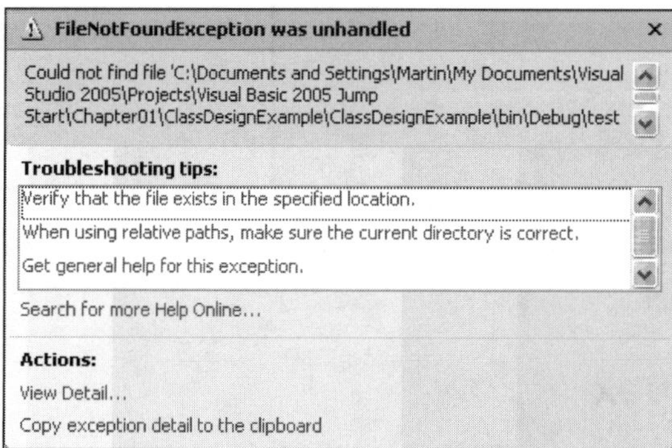

Figure 1-31 Troubleshooting tips from the Exception Assistant

Error Correction Dialog Box

When a design time error occurs, the syntax error is underlined with a red squiggly line. If you hover the mouse point over the error, the **Error Correction** dialog box offers suggestions on how to correct the error. In Figure 1-32 an attempt was made to assign a string variable to an integer variable. In Figure 1-33 the Error Correction dialog box suggests using CInt to convert the string into an integer. In this particular scenario it is a good solution to the problem.

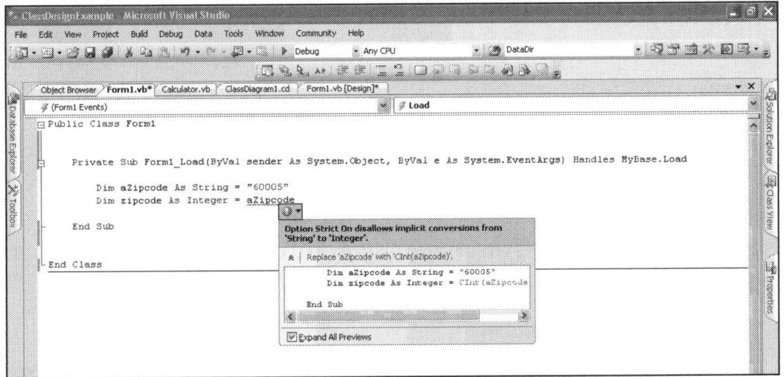

Figure 1-32 Using the Error Correction dialog box

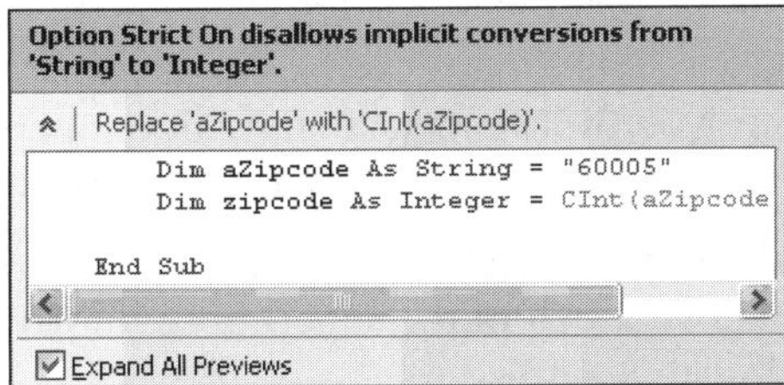

Figure 1-33 Recommendations from the Error Correction dialog box

Tracking Changes in the Editor

When a source file was changed in Visual Studio 2003, its tab in the Code Editor was marked with an asterisk. The problem was that there was no indication of what had changed. This often left people saying, "I don't remember making any changes, so I wonder what changed." In Visual Basic 2005 the changes are tracked and visually flagged both with an asterisk on the Classes tab in the Code Editor and also within the actual source file itself, as shown in Figure 1-34.

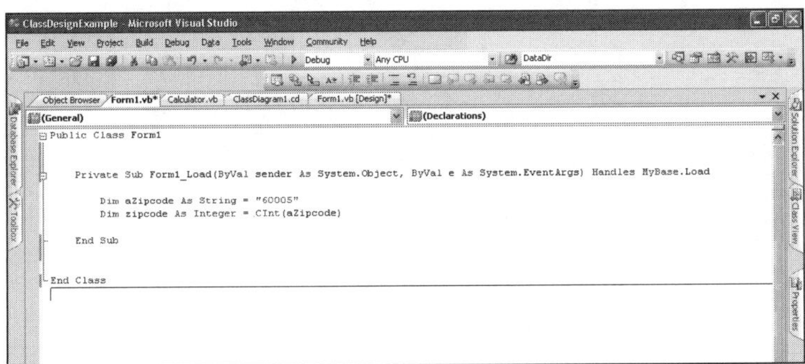

Figure 1-34 Showing the changes being tracked in a Visual Basic 2005 source file

Chapter Summary

This chapter explored the new features ofVisual Studio 2005 in the form of new designers, editors, panes, and dialogs.

- The Class Designer allows the classes of an application to be viewed visually. The Class Designer also allows methods, constants, events, and properties for a class to be easily defined and manipulated. New classes, interfaces, structures, and such can be defined using a drag-and-drop metaphor.
- The ObjectTest Bench is used in conjunction with the Class Designer to allow both instances and shared methods of classes to be invoked from the designer environment to test for correct functionality. This allows simple testing of a class's methods to occur within the Class Designer.
- The Settings pane of the Project Designer allows application and user settings to be easily defined and modified at design time.
- Refactoring will be a free download from Microsoft and will allow developers to easily make changes to existing code to make it more readable, reusable, and better structured.
- Debugger DataTips and visualizations allow easy access to relevant information about objects during a debugging session and remove much of the superfluous information that was displayed in Visual Studio .NET 2003 debugger.
- Edit and Continue allows changes to source code during a debugging session without the need to exit the debugger session to recompile and restart the debugger.
- Code snippets are a huge collection of well-organized prebuilt snippets of code that can be used to complete common programming tasks such as reading and writing files.
- The XML documentation you produce is used to automatically generate formatted HTML documentation.
- The Exception Assistant and Error Correction dialog boxes step up the amount of assistance provided by Visual Studio 2005 when a runtime exception or a design time syntax error occurs. Both provide guidance to the developer on how to fix the problem at hand.

CHAPTER

2

VISUAL BASIC 2005 LANGUAGE ENHANCEMENTS

In this chapter you will:

- See how My can make coding in Visual Basic 2005 much easier
- Explore new Visual Basic 2005 keywords
- Learn about new operators
- See how generics allows you to write better code
- Learn about the new application events
- Understand the value of new methods offered

This chapter covers language improvements in Visual Basic 2005. These enhancements can make application development easier, increase reuse, or just make life easier for you as you build your application. There are a number of major new capabilities that bring vast improvements to the Visual Basic language. The My feature allows developers to easily find the classes needed to complete a large number of common programming tasks without having intimate knowledge of the .NET Framework namespaces and the classes they contain. Generics offer all the type safety of arrays and all the flexibility and ease of use of collections. By using generics the developer can specify that a collection of strings is required and be sure that compiler ensures that only a collection of strings can be provided.

Application events make it possible to discover when your application is starting, ending, gaining or losing a network connection, experiencing an unhandled exception, or when more than one copy of the program is attempting to run.

Finally, a number of new keywords, operators, and the ability to perform operator overloading make Visual Basic more capable then its predecessors. All of these topics will be covered to allow you to get the most ofVisual Basic 2005.

My

Visual Basic 6.0 has an ease of use factor that Visual Basic .NET has not been able to match until Visual Basic 2005. As you learned in Chapter 1, Visual Basic 2005 adds a number of new features such as the Object Test Bench, Class Designer, and code snippets that make Visual Basic 2005 more powerful than any of its predecessors. Visual Basic 2005 also introduces a new Visual Basic Language feature called **My** that makes accomplishing routine programming tasks quite easy. One of the challenges of using Visual Basic has been that code has been broken into **namespaces**.

A namespace is simply a way of grouping classes together by their purpose. For example, all of the classes to perform file input and output (IO) operations are grouped in the System.IO namespace, and similarly all of the classes for building Windows Forms applications are in the System.Windows.Forms namespace. By grouping classes together by function it becomes easier to find the classes you need to perform a particular programming task.

Until you have some experience using namespaces, it is sometime tough to know where to look for the classes you need. For example, if you want to read a file you might guess the classes you need are in the System.IO namespace, but when you want to download files from the Internet it may not be obvious that the classes that are needed are in the System.Net namespace.

Have you ever been in a library or bookstore looking for a particular book, but had no idea where to find it? Thankfully, most of the time there is a helpful person behind the information counter who can help you find what you need. You can think of My as being a helpful person behind the information desk that can show you where the classes and methods you want are located.

For example, say you want to download a file from the Internet. The first step would be to figure out what namespace contained the class you need to accomplish this task. In Visual Basic .NET 2003, you would probably take a guess at the namespace that might contain the classes and methods needed to download a file. If that didn't work, you would resort to searching the online help. The following steps show how My can help:

1. In the Code Editor, type **My**. A context-menu with a list of choices appears, such as Application, Computer, and a few others.
2. Type **Computer**. The menu now offers more choices, as Figure 2-1 shows, one of which is Network.
3. The file is downloaded from a network, so this is an appropriate choice. Type **Network**.
4. Type **DownloadFile()**, which is the menu's first choice. Then supply a URL for the file to download to between the parentheses.

After these activities the line in the editor should look something like this:

```
My.Computer.Network.DownloadFile("http://www.microsoft.com")
```

2

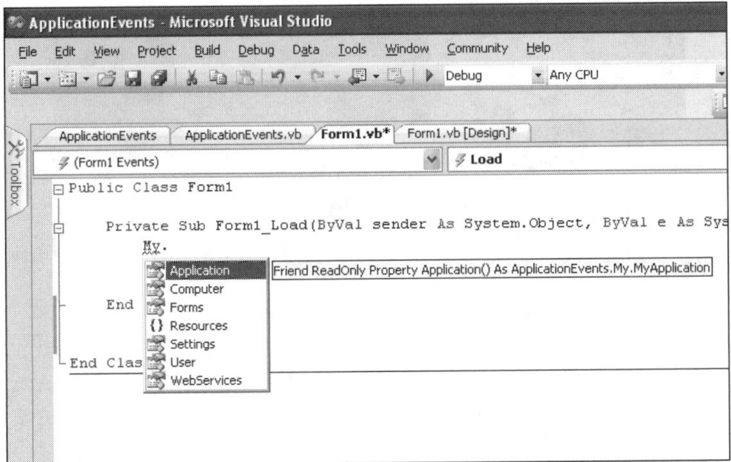

Figure 2-1 My Intellisense

Why use My? My helps a developer accomplish a task without knowing the namespace containing the classes he or she needs to accomplish the task. Additionally, My adds the Imports statements to easily access the required classes. If you know where the necessary classes are, you do not have to use My. My enhances **Intellisense** in Visual Basic 2005.

Intellisense is a context sensitive language reference that is built into the Code Editor in Visual Studio.

Table 2-1 lists the types of programming tasks that can easily be accomplished with My.

Table 2-1 My capabilities

My subcategory	My subcategory description
My.Application	Allows you to find out the following details about your application: • Application version number • If the application was deployed with ClickOnce • The command line the application was started with • A list of all open forms in the application • If the application saves user settings on application exit

Table 2-1 My capabilities (continued)

My subcategory	My subcategory description
My.Computer	Allows you to perform a number of programming tasks related to your computer such as: • Play an audio file • Read and write files • Access information about files, directories, and drives • Access the clipboard • Access serial ports • Access to the system Registry • Access to information about screen size and resolution
My.Forms	Allows easy access to all of the forms in the current application. My.Forms allows you to perform common programming tasks such as: • Open a new form • Communicate between forms (for example, get the value out of a TextBox on another form)
My.Resources	Allows easy access to application resources such as strings and images. My.Resources is used mostly in applications that are being internationalized. My.Resources allows easy access to the contents of resource files such as the following: • Images • Audio files • Strings • Icons
My.Settings	Can be used in conjunction with the Project Designer Settings pane to: • Retrieve user settings • Update user settings • Retrieve application settings
My. User	My.User allows easy access to information about a user, such as: • User login name • User domain name • Whether a user has logged in
My.WebServices	Allows easy access to any Web services that are part of a project and allows you to easily call Web services that are part of the current project

Intellisense is aware of My, so typing **My**. lists the different subcategories within My (Figure 2-1). The following sections provide helpful examples for using the functionality of each of the subcategories listed in Table 2-1.

My.Application

To help illustrate My.Application's functionality, examples and discussions of the following basic uses of **My.Application** are provided.

Obtain the Command Line for an Application

The For Each Next loop is used so that each separate argument on the command line is displayed. If there are no command line arguments, the For Each Next loop is skipped. This example writes the applications command line to the console:

```
' get the command line for this application
For Each cmd As String In _
    My.Application.CommandLineArgs

    Console.WriteLine("Commandline is " & cmd)
Next
```

Output:

```
Commandline is test.txt
```

Acquire the Application Version Number

The application version number is made up of four parts: the major version, major revision, minor version, and minor revision. This example writes the applications version to the console:

```
' get the version of this application
Dim verStr As String = _
  My.Application.Info.Version.ToString()

Console.WriteLine("The version is " _
  & verStr)
```

Output:

```
The version is 1.0.0.0
```

Retrieve the Company Name of a Publisher

Part of the information that is available in an application is the program developer's name. This example writes the program developer's name to the console:

```
' get the company name that produced this application
Dim companyStr As String = _
    My.Application.Info.CompanyName
Console.WriteLine("The software is made by " _
    & companyStr)
```

Output:

```
The software is made by SchraySoft
```

Capture the Application's Working Directory

Each application has a working directory. By default the application's working directory is the directory where the executable is located. This example writes the application's working directory to the console:

```
' get the working directory for this application
Dim dirStr As String = _
    My.Application.Info.DirectoryPath
Console.WriteLine("The working dir " _
    & dirStr)
```

Output:

```
The working dir C:\Documents and Settings\Martin\My
Documents\Visual Studio 2005\Projects\Visual Basic 2005 Jump
Start\Chapter02\ApplicationEvents\ApplicationEvents\bin\Debug
```

Set the SaveMySettingsOnExit Property

The SaveMySettingsOnExit property can be set to true or false. Setting it to true ensures that any changes to user settings while the application is running are saved and then the current setting is written out. This example sets SaveMySettingsOnExit to true and then displays the current value of SaveMySettingsOnExit to the console:

```
' save my setting when the application exits
My.Application.SaveMySettingsOnExit = True
Console.WriteLine("App settings will be saved " _
    & My.Application.SaveMySettingsOnExit)
```

Output:

```
Application settings will be saved True
```

Obtain the Application's Authentication Mode

An application can use the AuthenticationMode to check the type of authentication an application is using. This example writes a message to the console, indicating whether Windows or custom authentication is being used:

```
' check the authentication mode being used
Const msg As String = "This application is using "
If (My.Application.AuthenticationMode = _

ApplicationServices.AuthenticationMode.Windows) Then

    Console.WriteLine(msg & "Windows Authentication")
Else
    Console.WriteLine(msg & "custom Authentication")
End If
```

Output:

```
This application is using Windows Authentication
```

Retrieve the Value from the Environment homepath Variable

There is often useful information stored on a system in system environment variables. This example reads a value from the system environment variable named homepath and writes the value of homepath to the console:

```
' retrieve the value from the environment
' variable(HOMEPATH)
Dim strHomePath As String = _
    My.Application.GetEnvironmentVariable("HOMEPATH")
Console.WriteLine("HOMEPATH is " & strHomePath)
```

Output:

```
HOMEPATH is \Documents and Settings\Martin
```

Retrieve a List of Open Forms

This code retrieves a list of each form that is open in this application and prints their titles to the console:

```
' retrieve a list of each form that is
' open in this application and print its title
For Each f As Form In My.Application.OpenForms
    Console.WriteLine(f.Name & "'s title is " & f.Text)
Next
```

Output:

```
Form1's title is Form1
```

Determine if an Application Was Deployed Using ClickOnce

ClickOnce allows an application to easily be installed and updated from a network. ClickOnce is covered in Appendix A. This example determines if this application was deployed with ClickOnce, and then writes the appropriate message to the console:

```
' check if this application was deployed using ClickOnce
If (My.Application.IsNetworkDeployed) Then
    Console.WriteLine("This application was " & _
        "deployed using ClickOnce")
Else
    Console.WriteLine("This application was not " & _
        "deployed using ClickOnce")
End If
```

Output:

```
This application was not deployed using ClickOnce
```

My.Computer Examples

To help illustrate My.Computer's functionality, examples and discussions of the following basic uses of My.Computer are provided.

Find Where My Documents Is Located

Knowing the location of My Documents can be useful when a user is creating, reading, or writing files to his or her My Documents location in the file system. This example retrieves the location of My Documents and writes the value of homepath to the console:

```
' find where my document is located
Dim myDocPath As String = _
My.Computer.FileSystem.SpecialDirectories.MyDocuments

Console.WriteLine("My Documents is here " _
& myDocPath)
```

Output:

```
My Documents is here C:\Documents and Settings\Martin\My
Documents
```

Play a Sound File

This example checks to see if a sound file exists; if it does, the sound file is played. The reason for first checking to see if the sound file exists is that if it doesn't exist an exception occurs:

```
' check if a file exists and
' if so play the sound file
If (My.Computer.FileSystem.FileExists( _
"wez.wav")) Then
   My.Computer.Audio.Play("wez.wav")
End If
```

Result:

The sound file is played if the file exists.

Write a File

This example writes a string to the file named myfile.txt. If the file exists, the string is appended to the file:

```
' write a string to the file named myfile.txt and
' append to it if it exists
My.Computer.FileSystem.WriteAllText("myfile.txt", _
"Write this to a file", True)
```

Result:

The text `"Write this to a file"` is written into the myfile.txt file.

Play the System Beep Sound

This example causes the system beep sound to be played:

```
' play the beep built in system sounds
My.Computer.Audio.PlaySystemSound( _
    System.Media.SystemSounds.Beep)
```

Result:

The system beep sound is played.

Obtain the Current Date and Time

This example obtains the system date and time and displays it to the console:

```
' get the current date and time
Dim dateTime As Date = My.Computer.Clock.LocalTime
Console.WriteLine("Date/Time is " & _
      dateTime.ToString())
```

Output:

```
Date/Time is 7/5/2005 12:01:32 PM
```

Acquire a List of Networks

The following code retrieves a list of all file system drives. The two lines of code declare an array of type DriveInfo, make the size of the array equal to the number of system drives, and then copy the result from the My.Computer.FileSystem.Drives to the array. Next, a For Each Next loop is used to display each drive:

```
' get a list of all network drives
Dim drivesList(My.Computer.FileSystem.Drives.Count) _
      As IO.DriveInfo
My.Computer.FileSystem.Drives.CopyTo(drivesList, 0)

For Each drvInfo As IO.DriveInfo In drivesList
    If drvInfo IsNot Nothing Then
        MessageBox.Show(drvInfo.Name)
    End If
Next drvInfo
```

Output:

```
The system drives are
A:\
C:\
D:\
Y:\
Z:\
```

Retrieve Text from a Clipboard

This example examines the system clipboard to see if it contains text. If it does, all the text is copied from the clipboard and displayed in the system console:

```
' check if the clipboard contains text and if so
' display it
If (My.Computer.Clipboard.ContainsText) Then
    Console.WriteLine("Clipboard text")
    Console.WriteLine(My.Computer.Clipboard.GetText)
End If
```

Output:

```
Visual Basic Jump Start
```

List System Serial Ports

This example acquires a list of all system serial ports and displays them to the system console:

```
' list the serial ports
Console.WriteLine("System serial ports are:")
For Each prt As String In _
    My.Computer.Ports.SerialPortNames

    Console.WriteLine("Serial port: " & prt)
Next
```

Output:

```
System serial ports are:
Serial port: COM1
Serial port: COM2
```

Retrieve the CPU Name

This example reads the CPU name from the Registry and writes it to the console. Please see the Visual Basic 2005 online help for more information about the system Registry and reading and writing values to the Registry.

```
        ' read the CPU name from the registry
        Const KEYNAME As String = _
"HARDWARE\\DESCRIPTION\\SYSTEM\\CentralProcessor\\0"

        Dim regKey As Microsoft.Win32.RegistryKey
        regKey = _
My.Computer.Registry.LocalMachine.OpenSubKey(KEYNAME)

        If (regKey IsNot Nothing) Then
            Dim cpuStr As Object = _
regKey.GetValue("Identifier")
            Console.WriteLine("CPU " & cpuStr.ToString())
            regKey.Close()
        End If
```

Output:

```
CPU x86 Family 6 Model 13 Stepping 6
```

Obtain the Screen Size

This example obtains the screen width and height and displays them on the console:

```
' get the screen width and height
Dim width As Integer = _
    My.Computer.Screen.Bounds.Width
Dim height As Integer = _
    My.Computer.Screen.Bounds.Height
Console.WriteLine("Screen size is " & _
    width & " " & height)
```

Output:

```
Screen size is 1024 768
```

Acquire the Name of the Operating System

This example acquires the name of the operating system on the computer and writes it to the console:

```
' get the name of the operating system we are on
Console.WriteLine("OS Name " & _
    My.Computer.Info.OSFullName)
```

Output:

```
OS Name Microsoft Windows XP Professional
```

Check If the Shift Key Is Depressed

This example checks to see if the Shift key is depressed and displays true or false to the console, depending:

```
' check if the shift key is down
Console.WriteLine("The Shift Key is down " & _
        My.Computer.Keyboard.ShiftKeyDown)
```

Output:

```
The Shift Key is down False
```

Check for a Mouse Wheel

This example checks for the presence of a mouse wheel and displays the result to the console:

```
' check if the computer has a mouse with a wheel
If (My.Computer.Mouse.WheelExists) Then
    Console.WriteLine("This computer's mouse " & _
```

```
                "has a wheel")
        Else
            Console.WriteLine("This computer's mouse " & _
                "does not have a wheel")
        End If
```

Output:

```
This computer's mouse has a wheel
```

Download a File

This example downloads a file from a Web site and displays the file's size. In an effort to write more reliable code, the example also checks to see if there is a network connection and deletes any existing downloaded files if they exist.

Constants are used for the filename and site URL in the following example. The use of these constants makes the code more readable and easy to change. For example, if the filename or site URL changes, either needs to be changed in only one place in the program.

```
    ' make sure we have a network. If we do
    ' remove the existing download file and
    ' download a file
     If (My.Computer.Network.IsAvailable) Then

         Const FILENAME As String = "download.htm"
         Const SITEURL As String = _
             "http://www.martinschray.com/index.htm.hld"

         ' if the file already exists delete it
         If (My.Computer.FileSystem.FileExists(FILENAME)) _
         Then
             My.Computer.FileSystem.DeleteFile(FILENAME)
         End If

         ' download the file
         My.Computer.Network.DownloadFile(SITEURL, _
              FILENAME)

         Dim fileSize As Long = _
             My.Computer.FileSystem. _
             GetFileInfo(FILENAME).Length()
         Console.WriteLine("download file size is " & _
             fileSize)
     Else
         Console.WriteLine("Network is unavailable")
     End If
```

Output:

```
download file size is 7111
```

My.Forms Examples

My.Forms allows access to all of the forms in your application. Visual Studio is doing some work behind the scenes to generate code for My.Forms based on the actual forms that are in your project. Visual Studio looks at the actual forms that are in your project, as shown in Figure 2-2, and then configures Intellisense so it is aware of them.

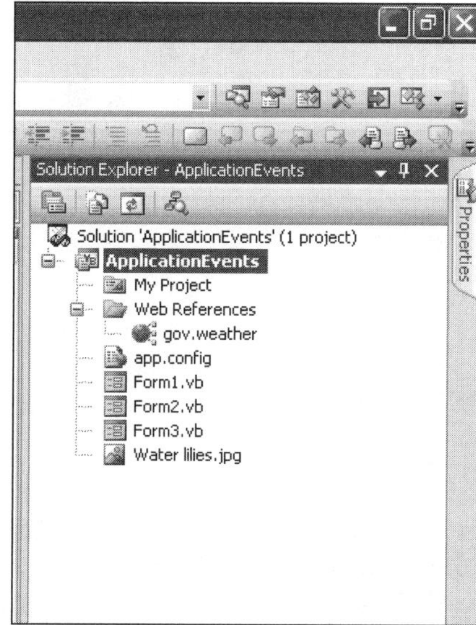

Figure 2-2 Forms that are part of this project: Form1, Form2, and Form3

The outcome is that only the forms that are part of your application show up in Intellisense when you access My.Forms. Figure 2-3 shows an example of Intellisense for a project that has three forms named Form1, Form2, and Form3.

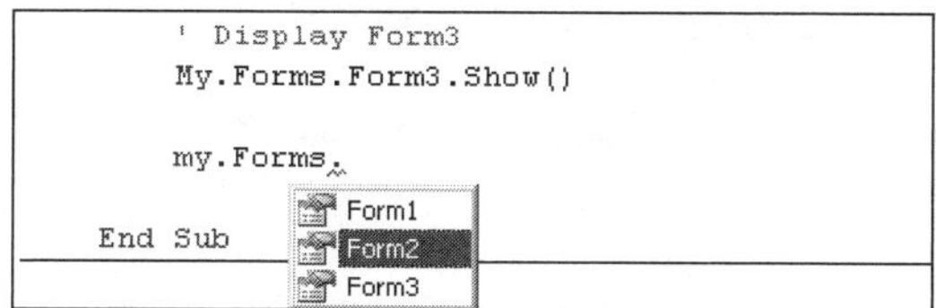

Figure 2-3 My.Forms Intellisense

The following examples show some of the capabilities of My.Forms in a project that contains Form1, Form2, and Form3.

Display the Title of Form2

This example displays the title of Form2:

```
' display the title of Form2
Console.WriteLine(My.Forms.Form2.Text)
```

Output:

```
Form2
```

Display Form2 as a Dialog Box

This example displays Form2 as a dialog box. Using ShowDialog causes a form to be displayed as a modal dialog box. This means that the user must close this form before he or she can get back to the application's main form.

```
' display Form2
Form2.ShowDialog()
```

Result:

This causes Form2 to be opened as a modal dialog box.

Access a Control on a Different Form

The goal of this example is to access a TextBox control on Form2 named txtZipcode from Form1. Note the use of the new String class function IsNullOrEmpty to easily check if a String is either null or empty. IsNullOrEmpty will be covered in more detail later in the chapter.

```
' access the form2's TextBox named txtZipcode
' and if its not empty display its value
If (Not String.IsNullOrEmpty( _
    My.Forms.Form2.txtZipcode.Text)) Then
    Dim zipCode As String = _
        My.Forms.Form2.txtZipcode.Text
    MessageBox.Show(zipCode, "Zipcode")
Else
    MessageBox.Show("Form2 Zipcode is empty", _
        "Zipcode empty")
End If
```

Output:

```
Form2 Zipcode is empty
```

Display a Form

The following example displays Form3:

```
' display Form3
My.Forms.Form3.Show()
```

Result:

This causes Form3 to be displayed.

My.Resources Examples

With **My.Resources**, you can access resources that have been extracted from an application. Typically, resources (strings, images, audio files, icons, and so on) are extracted from applications that are being internationalized. The basic idea is that everything in the application that might need to support a particular language or culture is extracted into resource files. In Visual Basic, resource files are just **Extensible Markup Language (XML)** files. An XML file is a file based on the conventions of the World Wide Web Consortium (W3C) XML standard. Chapter 1 has some examples of XML files in the Project Designer Settings pane. Each language or culture has its own file. By selecting a different resource file, different languages can be supported. Each item that is placed in a resource file has a unique identifier that allows you to retrieve that resource from the resource file.

Resource files can also be used to embed binary resources such as images, icons, and audio files. Rather than have images, icons, and audio files for the application loosely grouped into directories in the application, these resources can be embedded in resource files.

My.Resources can also access any resources that have been placed into resource files. Visual Studio 2005 generates code for each of the resources that you place into a resource file so that you can easily retrieve them by name. For example, if you have a resource that you named Form1_WelcomeLabel, you can simply refer to My.Resources.Form1_WelcomeLabel to retrieve it from the resource file as shown in the code snippet that follows. See Figure 2-4. An example of an image resource can be seen in Figure 2-5. Use the Project Designer Resource pane to add, delete, or maintain resources for your application. Figure 2-6 shows the various categories of resources available.

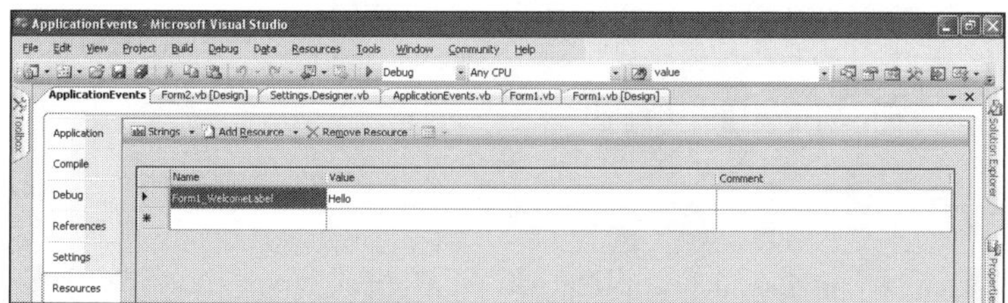

Figure 2-4 A String resource named Form1_WelcomeLabel

```
' get the value for the resource Form1_WelcomeLabel
Dim str As String = My.Resources.Form1_WelcomeLabel

MessageBox.Show(str)

' get the value for the resource Water_lilies
pbFlower.Image = My.Resources.Water_lilies
```

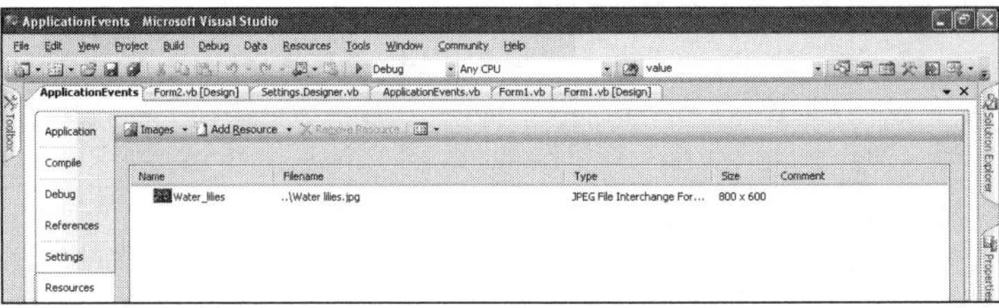

Figure 2-5 Image resource named Water_lilies

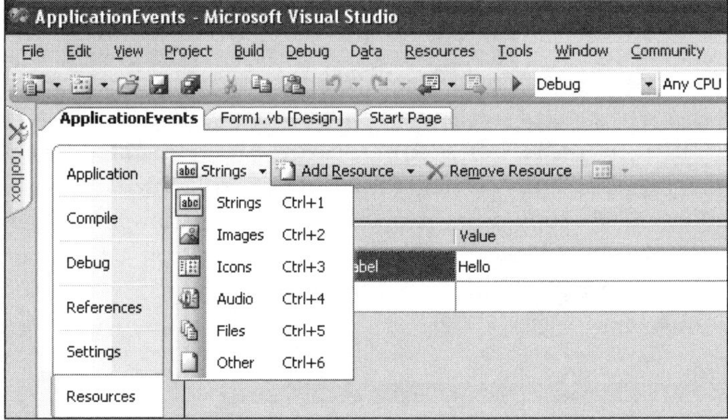

Figure 2-6 More types of supported resources

My.Settings

My.Settings allows you to access any application or user settings that are placed into the application's settings file, named app.config. Visual Studio 2005 generates code for each setting you add to your application via the Project Designer's Settings pane (see Chapter 1 for additional details), so that you can easily retrieve each setting by name. For example, if you have a setting that you named zipcode, shown in Figure 2-7, you can simply refer to My.Settings.zipcode to retrieve it from the settings file, as this example shows:

```
Dim zipcode As Integer = My.Settings.zipcode

MessageBox.Show(zipcode, "The Zipcode")
```

```
My.Settings.zipcode = 60005
My.Settings.Save()
```

Chapter 1 covered the fact that there are two kinds of settings supported in Visual Basic 2005. The first type are application settings, and the second type are user settings. My.Settings also gives you the ability to save user settings back to the settings file for any settings that have changed while the application is running. Application settings can only be read using My.Settings, and can't be modified and saved using My.Settings.

The application settings file is located in the project directory with the name app.config.

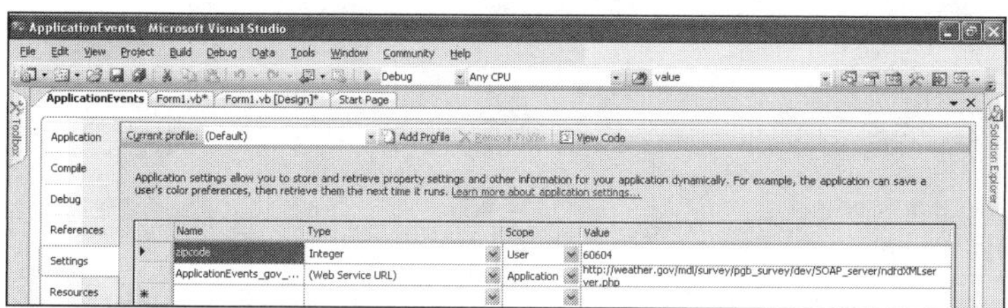

Figure 2-7 Application and user settings

My.User Examples

My.User provides information about the user. My.User provides important pieces of information relating to the identity of the user, whether the user is logged in, and the role of the user. The role of the user relates to the Windows operating system concept of users and groups. By default, the Windows operating system has a number of built-in roles such as Administrator, PowerUser, SystemOperator, User, and several other roles. Additionally you can add your own roles to the system. My.User is most useful when you are writing applications that are concerned with user identity, ensuring a user is logged in before he or she can use an application, or application security as it relates to user's identity.

This code uses My.User to carry out the following tasks related to the user:

- Checks if the user is an Administrator
- Checks if the user is authenticated (he or she logged in)
- Displays the user's name and domain

```
If (My.User.IsInRole( _
    ApplicationServices.BuiltInRole. _
    Administrator)) Then

    Console.WriteLine("Your role is Administrator")

End If

If (My.User.IsInRole("TestUser")) Then
```

```
            MessageBox.Show("You are a TestUser", _
                "Your Role is")

        End If

        ' check if the user is an autheticated user.
        ' If  they are provide a welcome message
        If (Not My.User.IsAuthenticated) Then
            Console.WriteLine("Only a logged in user " & _
            "can use this application")
        Else
            Dim user As String = My.User.Name
            Console.WriteLine("Welcome " & user)
        End If
```

Result:

Your role is Administrator

```
Welcome SchraySoft\Martin
```

My.WebServices Examples

My.WebServices makes it very easy to access any and all Web services that are available in any application. Although it is outside of the scope of this text to talk about the creation and use of Web services, it is important to understand what My.WebServices provides the programmer. My.WebServices allows you to access any Web service available within a project without adding any Imports directives to use the Web service.

In the following code, a call is made to the National Weather Service Web site. Please note that without adding the National Weather Service Web service to your project, this code won't be available in your project. This example is meant to show the capability of My.WebServices rather than provide a specific working example.

```
Dim latitude As Decimal = CDec(41.92522)
Dim longitude As Decimal = CDec(-88.18905)

Dim dateNow As DateTime = DateTime.Now

Dim dt As New DateTime(dateNow.Year, _
    dateNow.Month, dateNow.Day)

Dim weatherString As String = _
    My.WebServices.ndfdXML.NDFDgenByDay( _
    latitude, longitude, dt, "1", 1)
```

New Keywords

Keywords are not associated with any particular class or method but are basic building blocks for programming languages. Some examples of current keywords in Visual Basic are Dim, If, Then, Function, and Sub. Visual Basic 2005 adds the keywords Global, Using, and Continue.

Global

If you are creating your own namespaces and happen to use the same name as one of the existing .NET namespaces, the Visual Basic compiler won't be able to successfully compile. The following example illustrates a hierarchy in which the myProject.System namespace blocks access to the System namespace:

```
Namespace myProject
    Namespace system
        Class Student
            ' compile error can't find Long
            Function getValue() As System.Long
                ' compile error can't find Long
                Dim n As System.Long
                Return n
            End Function
        End Class
    End Namespace
End Namespace
```

As a result, the Visual Basic compiler cannot successfully resolve the reference to System.Long, because myProject.System does not define Long. To correct this problem you can use the new Global keyword. This allows you to specify the System namespace or any other namespace in the class library. The following example illustrates this:

```
Namespace myProject
    Namespace system
        Class Student
            Function getValue() As Global.System.Long
                Dim n As Global.System.Long
                Return n
            End Function
        End Class
    End Namespace
End Namespace
```

Using

The Using statement allows you to easily structure your code so that open resources such as files, network, or database connections are closed automatically. Any class that implements the IDisposable interface can be used with the Using keyword to ensure that the object is disposed of properly when the Using statement is complete. Any class that implements the IDisposable interface must provide a Dispose method. The Using statement ensures that the Dispose method is called to dispose of the object that was created with the Using keyword.

You certainly don't have to use the Using statement, but it can help ensure your application cleans up after itself.The examples below assume that Imports System.IO is placed at the top of the source file. In the code below, a file named test.txt is first opened for reading and then opened for writing. The following code throws an exception because the file is in use when the attempt is made to open the file for writing. This occurred because the StreamReader that was used to open the file was not closed before an attempt was made to open it for writing.

```
Const FILENAME As String = "test.txt"
Dim sr As New StreamReader(FILENAME)

Dim str As String = sr.ReadToEnd()

Dim sw As New StreamWriter(FILENAME, True)
sw.WriteLine("I am adding some text")
```

Although an obvious fix would be to simply close the StreamReader and StreamWriter, by incorporating a Using statement you ensure the StreamReader and StreamWriter are closed without the developer having to explicitly call the Close method. This example revises the example above to leverage the Using statement:

StreamReader and StreamWriter are not explicitly closed in the next code example. The Close method on the streams will be called automatically by the Using statement, so it is not necessary for the developer to do so.

```
Const FILENAME As String = "test.txt"

Using sr As New StreamReader(FILENAME)
    Dim str As String = sr.ReadToEnd()
End Using

Using sw As New StreamWriter(FILENAME)
    sw.WriteLine("I am adding some text")
End Using
```

Continue

Continue allows a programmer to easily skip to the next iteration of a loop. In the next example, if "i" is divisible by 4, then the control is passed to the While loop for the next iteration:

```
While i < 100
    i += 1
    If (i Mod 4 = 0) Then
        Continue While
```

```
        Else
            Console.WriteLine(i)
        End If
    End While
```

2

OPERATORS

Arithmetic and logical operators are critical building blocks in even the most basic programming in Visual Basic. Visual Basic 2005 introduces the ability to overload operators, which is an advanced Object Oriented Programming (OOP) technique. Additionally, a new logical operator named IsNot is introduced, making some logical comparisons much easier to read and write. The following section covers both operator overloading and the IsNot operator.

Overloading Operators

Arithmetic and logical operators can be overloaded. The same operator symbol can be overloaded with a new meaning. This means you as the programmer can define what >= or <= means to the class you are developing. This is referred to as operator overloading. **Operator overloading** is an advanced topic and could easily be the subject of an entire chapter, but this section briefly introduces this new capability of Visual Basic 2005. This is the first time that Visual Basic developers can overload basic logical operators such as =, >, <, and <> in their classes. The syntax is relatively straightforward, but the implication of overloading operator is not. For example, if you had a class named Person and overloaded the > operator, what would that really mean? To most people it would not be clear what a statement such as Person1 > Person2 really meant. Although operator overloading is a powerful option, you have to consider whether overloading an operator makes your code clearer and easier to understand. Arguably, some operators such as <> and = are probably clearer because they refer to equality or inequality when comparing two objects.

In addition to the operator overloading described above, there are several special operators that can be overloaded. The operators IsTrue, IsFalse, Not, and CType can be overloaded. The operators IsTrue and IsFalse can't be called directly from your code, but the compiler does use them. For example, in the following code, the compiler actually calls p1.IsTrue() when it evaluates the If statement.

```
If (p1) Then
    MessageBox.Show("p1 Isnot nothing", "person")
End If
```

The next example combines the overloading of <>, =, IsTrue, IsFalse, Not, and CType in a single class named Person. This example is meant to provide a basic idea of the capabilities that operator overloading can provide.

If you overload an operator, you must overload its counterpart operator also. For example, if you overload <>, the compiler requires you to overload = as well. If you overload >, the compiler requires you to overload < as well.

```
Public Class Person

    Private firstName, lastName As String

    Public Sub New(ByVal firstName As String, _
    ByVal lastName As String)
        Me.firstName = firstName
        Me.lastName = lastName
    End Sub


    Public Shared Operator <>(ByVal person1 As Person, _
        ByVal person2 As Person) As Boolean

        ' checking that they are NOT equal
        If (person1.lastName = person2.lastName) And _
            (person1.firstName = person2.firstName) Then
            Return False
        End If

        Return True
    End Operator

    Public Shared Operator =(ByVal person1 As Person, _
    ByVal person2 As Person) As Boolean

        ' checking that they are equal
        If (person1.lastName = person2.lastName) And _
            (person1.firstName = person2.firstName) Then
            Return True
        End If

        Return False
    End Operator

    Public Shared Operator IsTrue(ByVal obj As Person) As Boolean
        If obj IsNot Nothing Then
            Return True
        Else
            Return False
        End If
    End Operator
```

```
    Public Shared Operator IsFalse(ByVal obj As Person) As
Boolean
        Return Not obj
    End Operator

    Public Shared Operator Not(ByVal obj As Person) As Boolean
        If obj Then
            Return False
        Else
            Return True
        End If
    End Operator

    Public Shared Widening Operator CType(ByVal obj As
Person) As String
        Return obj.firstName & " " & obj.lastName
    End Operator

End Class
```

The following code makes use of the Person class and tests some of the functionality of the person class:

```
        Dim p1 As New Person("Bob", "Sled")
        Dim p2 As New Person("Bob", "Sled")
        Dim p3 As Person = Nothing
        Dim p4 As New Person("Fred", "Smith")

        If (p1 = p2) Then
            Console.WriteLine("p1 and p2 objects are equal")
        End If

        If (p1 <> p4) Then
            Console.WriteLine("p1 and p4 objects are NOT
Equal")
        End If

        Dim str As String = CType(p1, String)
        Console.WriteLine("Name is " & str)

        If (p1) Then
            Console.WriteLine("p1 IsNot Nothing")
        End If

        If (Not p3) Then
            Console.WriteLine("p3 is Nothing")
        End If
    End Sub
```

Output:

```
p1 and p2 objects are equal
p1 and p4 objects are NOT Equal
Name is Bob Sled
p1 IsNot Nothing
p3 is Nothing
```

IsNot

IsNot is a handy addition to the Visual Basic family of logical operators. Historically you would have to use some confusing code to take action if an object was not equal Nothing. The following example shows this:

```
If (Not obj Is Nothing) Then
    MessageBox.Show("obj <> nothing", _
      "Obj has a value")
End If
```

Just reading the If statement "If not obj Is Nothing" is pretty confusing. Wouldn't it be easier if you could just code the statement to say "If obj IsNot Nothing"? The authors of Visual Basic 2005 thought so and added IsNot for just this situation, as the next example illustrates:

```
If (obj IsNot Nothing) Then
    MessageBox.Show("obj <> nothing", _
      "Obj has a value")
End If
```

Generics, Collections, and Arrays

Arrays, **collections**, and **generics** each allow you to do the same basic thing—store data types, such as **Integer** and **String**, in memory as a group. Generics are a way of defining strongly typed collections and are one of the new language features in .NET Framework 2.0. Because generics are implemented in the **Common Language Runtime (CLR)**, they are available to all .NET languages (such as VB. NET and C#).

Strongly typed means that when a variable is declared, it can only be assigned certain types of values based on the declared data type. An example of this is when you declare an Integer and assign it a value. The compiler ensures that you can assign only Integer values to this variable.

There are differences in the way that arrays, collections, and generics accomplish this task. Collection classes and generic collection classes automatically add capacity (resize) when they become full. However, arrays must be manually resized by a developer. Arrays and generics are strongly typed but collections are not. Table 2-2 compares the features of arrays, collections, and generics.

2

Table 2-2 Comparing arrays, collections, and generics

Data type storage mechanism	Strongly typed	Automatic resizing
Arrays	Yes	No; the developer must manually redimension the array
Collection classes	No	Yes
Generics	Yes	Yes

Arrays

Arrays are strongly typed. When an array is declared, the data type must be specified as part of the declaration:

```
Dim MyStringArray(10) As String
```

In this statement, an array named MyStringArray is declared as an array of strings. Because arrays are strongly typed, as items are assigned to the array they are first checked by the compiler to see if they are of the String data type. If they are not, a compile error is generated. Figure 2-8 shows the compiler message indicating that an Integer cannot implicitly be converted to a String due to use of the option strict.

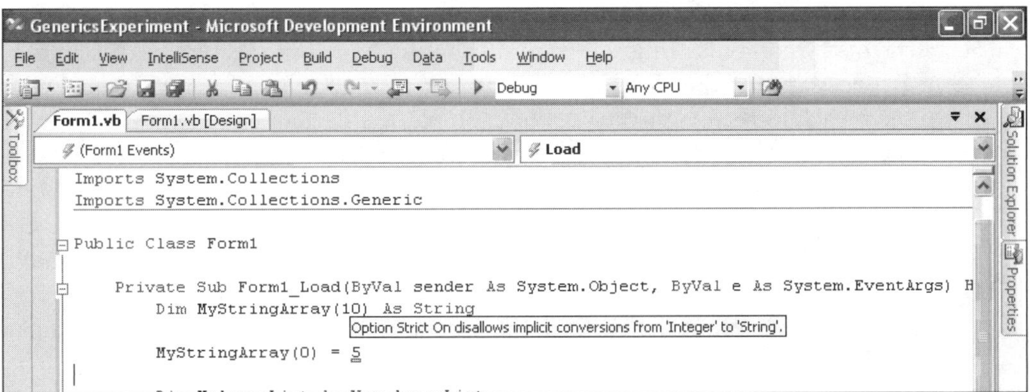

Figure 2-8 Arrays are strongly typed

Many would argue that the big issue with arrays is that they have a fixed size. If an array is declared to hold 10 elements and an additional element needed to be added to the array, the array would have to be redimensioned. The ReDim keyword can be used to increase the size of the array. Using the ReDim keyword in conjunction with the Preserve keyword preserves the contents of the array as it is resized. Arrays have the benefit of being strongly typed but must be manually resized by the developer.

Collections

Collections classes (ArrayList, Stack, Queue, and so on) are not strongly typed, but they are by their nature automatically resizable. Collections are essentially resizing containers that increase in size automatically as more elements are added to them. Given that collections classes (e.g., ArrayList) resize automatically, why would someone choose to use an array? Collections are not strongly typed, so any data type can be added to them. The following example shows why strong typing is so important:

```
Dim MyArrayList As New ArrayList

MyArrayList.Add("Fred")
MyArrayList.Add(5)
MyArrayList.Add(New Person()
```

Here, a new ArrayList named MyArrayList was declared and created. Note in the declaration that there is no way to specify the data type the ArrayList can accept. So, for example, there is no way to specify that this collection accepts only Strings. The example code above adds a String, an Integer, and a Person object to MyArrayList. As this example shows, because the ArrayList is not strongly typed it accepts any data type. So what is the issue?

Remember that ArrayList treats everything like an object. When any object is retrieved from the ArrayList, it is returned as a System.Object type. If the developer adds a String to the ArrayList, when the String is retrieved from the ArrayList it is returned as an Object. Often it is necessary for the developer to convert (using Ctype) or cast (using DirectCast) the Object back to the original type. For example, the developer adds a String to the ArrayList. When the developer retrieves the String from the ArrayList, it is returned as type Object. If the developer wants to call any String functions, the returned Object must be placed back into a String object using either CType or DirectCast. CType will assume the Object is not a string and attempt to convert the Object to a String. DirectCast will assume the Object already contains a String object and won't attempt a conversion. The developer writes the following code using a For Each statement to grab each individual String out of the ArrayList:

```
For Each str As String In MyArrayList
    'Perform desired processing on each item.
    Console.WriteLine(str)
Next str
```

The For Each statement automatically converts the data it extracts based on the data type specified in the For Each declaration. In this example, str As String, instructs the For Each to cast the data to a String. The problem is that MyArrayList doesn't just contain strings, so an InvalidCastException is generated, as Figure 2-9 illustrates.

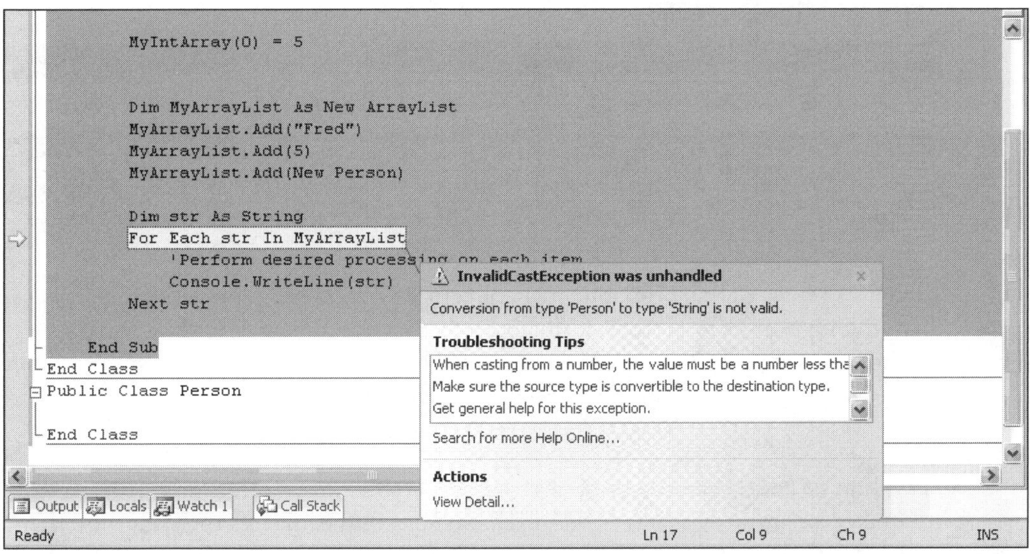

Figure 2-9 Collections are not strongly typed, and so runtime exceptions can occur

The issue is that although collections classes accept any data type, the code using the collections classes is usually expecting a certain data type. One solution is to check the type of each item as it is pulled out of the ArrayList. A better solution would be to allow only the correct data types to be added to the collections. That is exactly what generics do.

Generics

Generics are a way of making collections strongly typed. In the past, the only way to make a strongly typed collection was to inherit from CollectionBase and build a custom collection class. If you want a type-safe collection for Integer and Long, you need to build two new collections inherited from CollectionBase. In fact, for each data type that a type-safe collection was required for, it would be necessary to inherit from CollectionBase and build a type-safe collection by hand. That could end up being a lot of work.

What enables generics to be type safe and allows you to avoid inheriting from Collection-Base for every data type you want a type-safe collection for? The compiler generates the appropriate classes based on the data type that is specified in the generic collection declaration. Table 2-3 provides the list of collection classes that support generics in Visual Basic 2005.

Table 2-3 Generic collections

Collection	Description
SortedDictionary	Accepts keys and values and maintains them in sorted order
Dictionary	Accepts keys and values, but the order is not maintained
List	Accepts objects and stores them
Queue	Accepts objects and stores them in a First In First Out (FIFO) queue
Stack	Accepts objects and stores them in a Last In First Out (LIFO) stack

Generics provide all the flexibility of collections and all the type safety of arrays. Generics are basically type-safe collections. Unlike the declaration of the ArrayList, the declaration of any of the generic collection types requires that the data type that the generic collection can accept must be part of the declaration. The following code illustrates this concept:

```
Dim MyStringList As New List(Of String)
```

This line of code declares a new list named MyStringList. Note that the constructor of the List takes an argument that contains Of String. This indicates the data type that MyStringList accepts. Virtually any data types or classes can be used as the argument to the generic collection constructor.

A compile error occurs if someone tries to add anything other than a String to MyStringList. In the collections example in Figure 2-9, an exception occurs when the application runs (a runtime error); with generics you have strong typing in place so this problem would be caught at compile time, as shown in the following example:

```
Dim MyStringList As New List(Of String)

MyStringList.Add("a")
MyStringList.Add("b")
MyStringList.Add(5)     ' COMPILE ERROR

For Each str As String In MyStringList
    'perform desired processing on each item.
    Console.WriteLine(str)
Next str
```

When this code is compiled, the compiler flags the line of code attempting to add an Integer to the list (MyStringList.Add(5)) as an error. Once a collection class that supports generics (Dim MyStringList As New List(Of String)) is declared to accept a particular type (e.g., String), the compiler allows only data of that data type to be added to the collection. Figure 2-10 illustrates error information the compiler provides when an attempt to add invalid data type to a list is made.

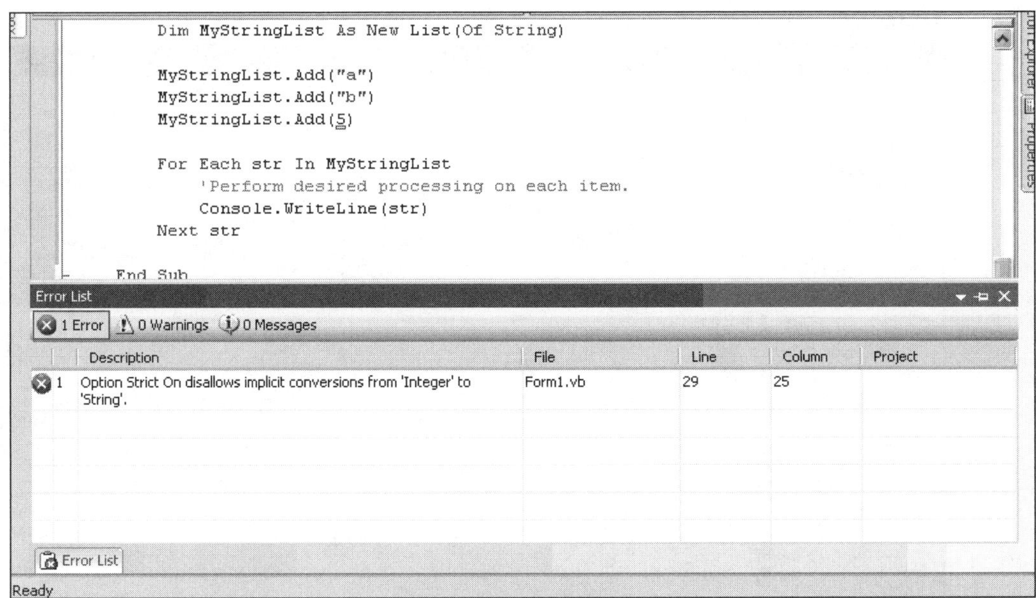

Figure 2-10 Compiler error for invalid type assignment

Option explicit is an option that can be turned on and off. When on, **implicit conversions** are not allowed, meaning in a situation where conversation needs to take place, a compile error is thrown. For example, if option explicit were turned off for the application in Figure 2-10, the Integer would automatically be converted to a String. It is always recommended to turn option explicit on because you probably want to make the decision yourself and not have the compiler do it for you. After all, the compiler has to guess what you intended to happen.

New Application Events

There are a number of events that occur as a program runs that you, as a programmer, should be aware of. Typically you might be interested when your application starts so that you can load application data or when an application ends so that you can save application data. Visual Basic defines five application events. You can add code to your application so that you are notified when any of these five events occur. Table 2-4 lists all application events along with a brief description of each event.

Table 2-4 Application events

Application event	Event description
Startup	This event occurs when your application is started. This event can be used to load application data such as a list of states when the application loads.
Shutdown	This event occurs when your application is being shut down. This event can be used to save application data such as data the user has edited, but has not yet saved.
UnhandledException	This event allows you to catch any unhandled exception that your application throws. For example, if your application has an exception and has no Try Catch blocks to handle the exception, an uncaught exception has occurred.
StartupNextInstance	The StartupNextInstance event occurs if there is a copy of your application running and there is an attempt to start another copy. This event occurs only if the make this application single instance checkbox is checked (see the Project Designers Application pane; see Chapter 1).
NetworkAvailabilityChanged	The NetworkAvailabilityChanged event occurs only if there is a change in network availability. This event won't occur unless there is a change in network availability.

In Visual Basic there are literally hundreds of events that are generated as an application is running. These events are caused by activities such as moving the mouse, hitting a key, controls gaining and losing focus, typing characters in a TextBox, or making a selection from a Listbox. Rather than making you aware of every event that occurs, Visual Basic allows you to add code to indicate that your code handles a particular event. Application events require you to add code and indicate that your code handles the various application events.

Setting up Application Events

To access an application event for the first time, you need to complete the following steps.

1. Press **Ctrl+Alt+L**, or from the VS.NET 2005 menu bar, choose **View**, and then **Solution Explorer** to open Solution Explorer.
2. Once Solution Explorer is visible, right-click the project and click **Properties**, as shown in Figure 2-11. This opens the Project Designer.
3. Select the **Application** pane in the Project Designer as shown in Figure 2-12.
4. Click the **View Application Events** button, also shown in Figure 2-12.

Having completed this series of steps, the ApplicationEvents.vb file opens in Visual Studio and allows you to view the MyApplication class. The next step is to add code to handle the application events that you are interested in.

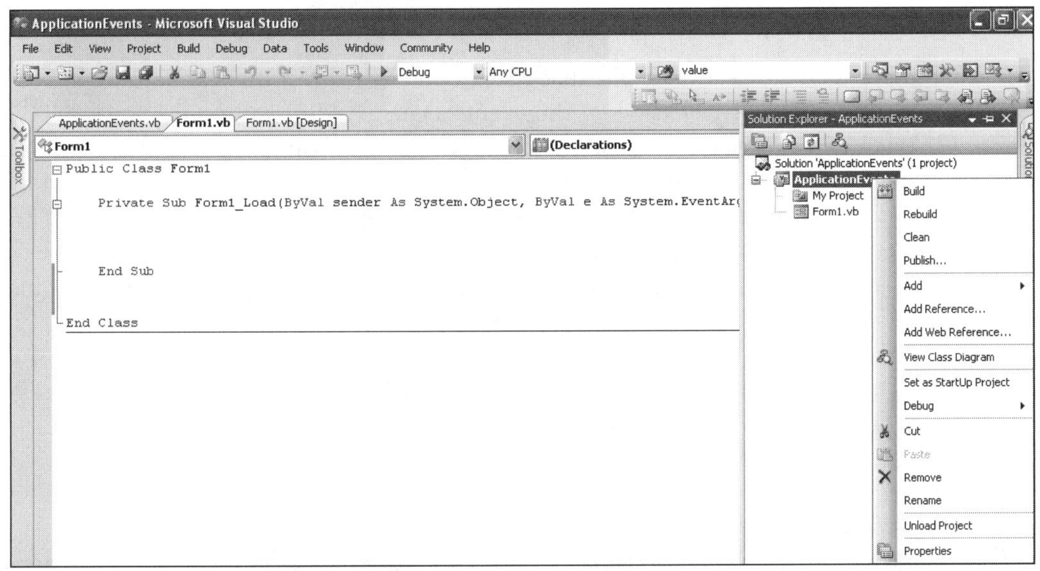

Figure 2-11 Opening the Project Designer

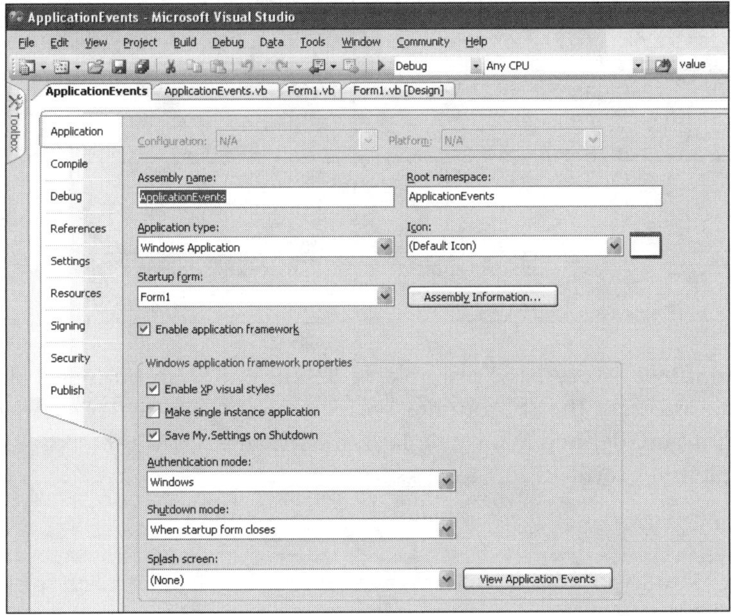

Figure 2-12 The Project Designer Application pane

Registering Application Events

If there is an application event that you are interested in, you will have to add a subroutine to your code to be called when the event occurs. Additionally, once you have declared the subroutine, you have to indicate that this subroutine handles the application event. This is done by adding a Handles keyword to the end of the subroutine declaration. This indicates that the subroutine handles that event. The only piece of this that gets a bit tricky is determining which arguments each subroutine must be declared with. Each application event uses different arguments based on the type of application event. Table 2-5 lists application events and their required arguments.

The good news is that if you are not interested in a particular application event there is no action required.

Table 2-5 Application events and their required arguments

Application Event	Argument#1	Argument#2
Startup	sender As System.Object	Microsoft.VisualBasic. ApplicationServices. StartupEventArgs
Shutdown	sender As System.Object	System.EventArgs
UnhandledException	sender As System.Object	Microsoft.VisualBasic. ApplicationServices. UnhandledExceptionEventArgs
StartupNextInstance	sender As System.Object	Microsoft.VisualBasic. ApplicationServices. StartupNextInstanceEventArgs
NetworkAvailability-Changed	sender As System.Object	Microsoft.VisualBasic.Devices. NetworkAvailableEventArgs

The following code shows a very basic example of defining the subroutines and using the Handles keyword to associate the subroutines with the event they will be called for. All subroutine declarations are defined as a single line of code in VB, but the code below must be shown in multiple lines to fit in this text.

```
    Class MyApplication

        Public Sub AppStartup(ByVal sender As System.Object,
            ByVal e As
Microsoft.VisualBasic.ApplicationServices.StartupEventArgs)
            Handles MyBase.Startup

            MessageBox.Show("I am starting")

        End Sub

        Public Sub AppShutdown(ByVal sender As System.Object,
```

```
        ByVal e As System.EventArgs) Handles MyBase.Shutdown

        MessageBox.Show("I am shutting down")
    End Sub

    Public Sub AppUnhandledException(ByVal sender As System.
Object,
        ByVal e As Microsoft.VisualBasic.ApplicationServices.
UnhandledExceptionEventArgs)
        Handles MyBase.UnhandledException

        MessageBox.Show("Unhandeled Exception")

    End Sub

    Public Sub AppStartupNextInstance(ByVal sender As System.
Object,
        ByVal e As Microsoft.VisualBasic.ApplicationServices.
StartupNextInstanceEventArgs)
        Handles MyBase.StartupNextInstance

        MessageBox.Show("Another instance is starting")
    End Sub

    Public Sub AppNetworkAvailabilityChanged(ByVal sender As
System.Object,
        ByVal e As Microsoft.VisualBasic.Devices.
NetworkAvailableEventArgs)
        Handles MyBase.NetworkAvailabilityChanged

        MessageBox.
Show("Network availability changed, network is available:  " & e.
IsNetworkAvailable)
    End Sub
End Class
```

New Methods

There are a number of new classes and classes with new methods available in Visual Basic 2005. Although there are several candidates for inclusion in this section, there are two major topics that really stand out. The first is how to convert string data into numeric data, and the second is determining if a String is equal to Nothing or if it is an empty String.

Converting Strings to Numbers

Visual Basic .NET provided two major ways to convert string data to numeric data. The first way was to use a method such as Integer.Parse or Decimal.Parse, depending on whether the string represented a whole number or decimal. The second approach was to use the Convert class and one of its methods, such as ToInt32 or ToDecimal. The problem with these approaches was that if the conversion failed, it threw an exception. Rather than writing code to catch an exception, most people wanted a simple way to tell if the conversion had succeeded or failed:

```
        Try
            zipcode = Integer.Parse(txtZipcode.Text)
            MessageBox.Show(zipcode.ToString(), _
"zipcode is")
        Catch ex As Exception
            MessageBox.Show(txtZipcode.Text, _
"Invalid Zipcode")
        End Try
```

Additionally, if you attempted a conversion without a Try Catch block and the conversion failed, your application would have an uncaught exception.

Visual Basic 2005 adds a method called **TryParse** to numeric data types such as Integer, Decimal, and Short. TryParse takes two arguments: the first is a String to be converted and the second is a variable to store the converted value in. The TryParse method returns a Boolean value to indicate success or failure of the conversion.

TryParse is more efficient than Parse because it does not have to go through the overhead of throwing an exception.

The following code shows an example of using TryParse to attempt the conversion of a string from a TextBox control named txtZipcode.

```
Dim zipcode As Integer

If (Integer.TryParse(txtZipcode.Text, zipcode)) Then
    MessageBox.Show(zipcode.ToString(), "zipcode is")
Else
    MessageBox.Show(txtZipcode.Text, "Invalid Zipcode")
End If
```

Checking for Empty or Nothing Strings

When using strings it is common to check to see if the String is either Nothing or empty. In the following code, there are two checks that are going on in the If statement: the first checks if the String is Nothing, and the second checks to see if the String is equal to String.Empty.

```
If (zipcode Is Nothing Or zipcode=String.Empty) Then
    Console.WriteLine("string is empty or null")
Else
    Console.WriteLine("string has value")
End If
```

The String class has a new, shared method named IsNullOrEmpty. In case you are wondering, null is just another way of saying it is equal to Nothing. This example shows that by using IsNullOrEmpty, only a single condition needs to be checked, thus simplifying the code required for the check:

```
If (String.IsNullOrEmpty(zipcode)) Then
    Console.WriteLine("string is empty or null")
Else
    Console.WriteLine("string has value")
End If
```

CHAPTER SUMMARY

This chapter explored the new language features in Visual Studio 2005.

- My makes routine programming tasks easier in a number of categories such as getting information about the application; accessing such resources as files and directories, serial ports, and drives (disk, floppy, CD, and such) and forms in an application; obtaining information about the user of the application; accessing all the forms in the application; accessing settings and resources in the application; and calling Web services.
- Visual Basic 2005 includes new keywords including Global, Using, and Continue that enhance Visual Basic 2005 language.
- Visual Basic 2005 adds the IsNot operator and for the first time allows operator overloading for the <, >, <>, and = operators, among others. Additionally, the special operators CType, IsTrue, IsFalse, and Not can now be overridden.
- Generics have the ease of use of collections but add the safety of strong typing, thus making generic collections easy and type safe.
- Application events allow you to get information about when your application starts, stops, has unhandled exceptions, or gains or loses network connections.

CHAPTER

3

ENHANCEMENTS TO WINDOWS FORMS APPLICATIONS

In this chapter you will:

- Learn about the new Common Controls, Containers, and Menus and Toolbars categories in the Toolbox
- Review the capabilities of the new MaskedTextBox and WebBrowser Common Controls
- See examples using the FlowLayoutPanel, TableLayoutPanel, and Split-Container Containers to build an application that gracefully resizes windows
- Gain an appreciation for enhancements to Menus & Toolbars
- Discover the new BackgroundWorker and SerialPort components

Visual Basic 2005 improves the developer's ability to quickly build sophisticated and visually appealing applications with new controls, containers, and components. The first change is how controls are organized in the Toolbox (Figure 3-1). With the addition of new controls and new types of controls, the designers of Visual Basic 2005 felt it was necessary to organize the Toolbox into of the following major categories to make easier to find needed items from the Toolbox:

- Common Controls
- Containers
- Menus and Toolbars
- Data
- Components
- Printing
- Dialogs
- General

Depending on the edition of Visual Studio 2005 that you are using (and its configuration), you may see additional categories, such as Dialog Editor, Dataset, WebParts, and others.

Common Controls, Containers, and Menus and Toolbars are covered in depth throughout the chapter, while a few new additions to the components of the Toolbox are covered briefly at the end of this chapter.

The exciting changes that greatly expand Visual Basics capabilities to access data will be covered in Chapter 6. The Printing, Dialogs, and General categories are pretty much as they were in the past.

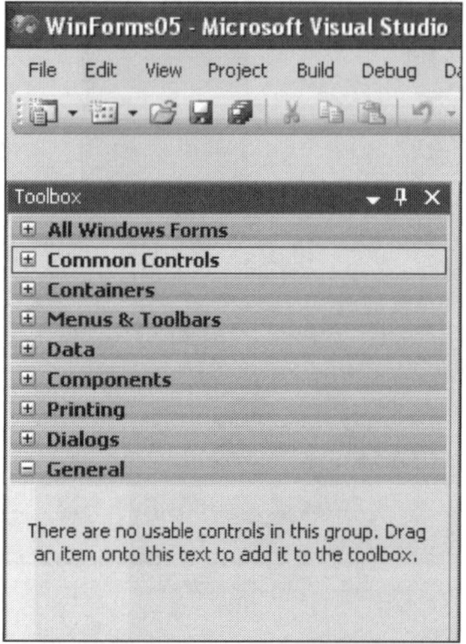

Figure 3-1 The Toolbox has a number of tabs to assist with organizing controls

Common Controls

There are two extremely useful common controls that have resurfaced in Visual Basic 2005. The first control is MaskedTextBox, which was a very popular control in Visual Basic 6.0, but had been missing from recent versions of Visual Basic, until Visual Basic 2005.

The second control is WebBrowser, which has been around in the form of an Active X control for quite some time. Visual Basic 2005 provides a WebBrowser control that is more full featured and offers much better integration with .NET Framework.

Additionally, controls such as TextBox and ComboBox have been enhanced to support the AutoComplete feature. This allows a list of possible choices to be offered as the user types text into the control.

MaskedTextBox Control

Have you ever needed to have a user enter data in a specific format, such as a phone number? In essence, what is required is a visual clue for the user, so they know the expected format of the data. Additionally, it would be great to allow the user to enter only valid data. The basic purpose of the **MaskedTextBox** is to provide the user with visual clues on what valid data looks like and to enforce validation rules so that only valid data is entered. For example, a MaskedTextBox is used in Figure 3-2 to provide a user with a visual clue as well as a template for entering a phone number. If the user attempts to enter data that is not numeric or does not comply with the makeup of a phone number, the data does not appear in the MaskedTextBox. Figure 3-3 shows the MaskedTextBox after successful data entry.

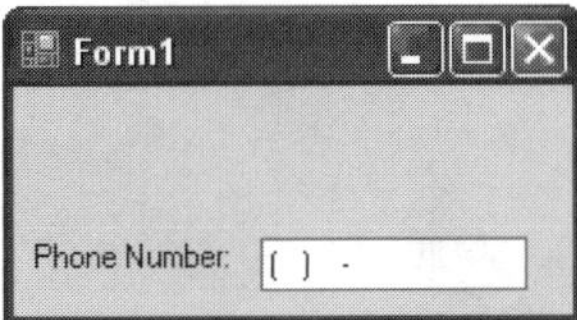

Figure 3-2 MaskedTextBox with phone number mask

Figure 3-3 MaskedTextBox with a valid phone number

Given the fact that the MaskedTextBox has been missing from Visual Basic since Visual Basic 6.0, most developers would use a **TextBox** in this situation. The issue with using a TextBox is that there is no generic way of validating user input as a user enters that data. This usually means that the user enters all his or her data and then the data is validated. By using the MaskedTextBox, it is clearer to the user what he or she should be entering, and the mask ensures that only valid data can be entered.

The MaskedTextBox supports a number of predefined masks and also allows custom masks to be specified. Figure 3-4 shows the predefined templates that are included with the MaskedTextBox. Masks can be set up by right clicking a MaskedTextBox control, selecting its properties, and then clicking the ellipsis next to the Mask property (Figure 3-5). Additionally, the mask property can be set from code. In the following example, the MaskedTextBox, named mtbPhoneNumber, has its mask set so that it can accept area codes and phone numbers:

```
mtbPhoneNumber.Mask = "(999) 000-0000"
```

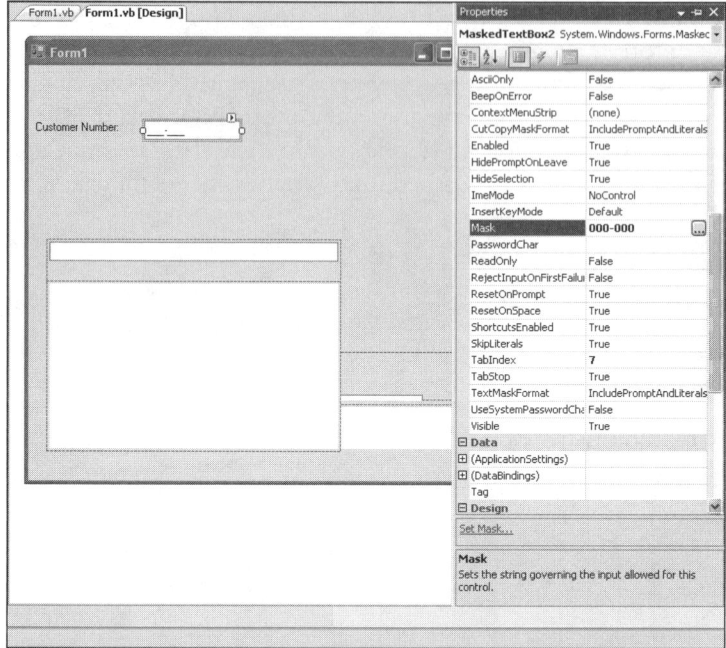

Figure 3-4 List of standard Input masks for the MaskedTextBox

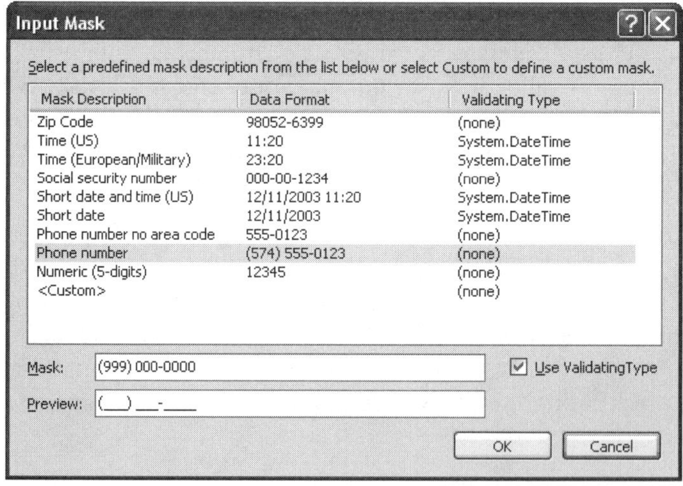

Figure 3-5 Specifying an edit mask for the MaskedTextBox

Table 3-1 was reproduced from the Visual Studio 2005 help system and shows the elements that can be used to make up a valid mask for the MaskedTextBox control.

Table 3-1 Valid edit mask elements

Mask element	Description
0	Digit, entry required; this element accepts any single digit between 0 and 9.
9	Digit or space, entry optional
#	Digit or space, entry optional. If this position is left blank in the mask, it is rendered as a space in the Text, InputText, and OutputText properties. Plus (+) and minus (–) signs are allowed.
L	Letter, entry required. Restricts input to the ASCII letters a–z and A–Z. This mask element is equivalent to [a-zA-Z] in regular expressions.
?	Letter, entry optional. Restricts input to the ASCII letters a–z and A–Z. This mask element is equivalent to [a-zA-Z]? in regular expressions.
&	Character, entry required; if the AsciiOnly property is set to true, this element behaves like the *L* element.
C	Character, entry optional. Any noncontrol character. If the AsciiOnly property is set to true, this element behaves like the *?* element.
A	Alphanumeric, entry optional; if the AsciiOnly property is set to true, the only characters it accepts are the ASCII letters a–z and A–Z.
.	Decimal placeholder; the actual display character used will be the decimal placeholder appropriate to the current UI culture, as determined by the control's Culture property.
,	Thousands placeholder; the actual display character used will be the thousands placeholder appropriate to the current culture, as determined by the control's Culture property.
:	Time separator; the actual display character used will be the time placeholder appropriate to the current culture, as determined by the control's Culture property.
/	Date separator; the actual display character used will be the date placeholder appropriate to the current culture, as determined by the control's Culture property.
$	Currency symbol; the actual character displayed will be the currency symbol appropriate to the current culture, as determined by the control's Culture property.
<	Shift down; converts all characters that follow to lowercase
>	Shift up; converts all characters that follow to uppercase
|	Disables a previous shift up or shift down
\	Escape. Escapes a mask character, turning it into a literal. "\\" is the escape sequence for a backslash.
All other characters	Literals. All nonmask elements will appear as themselves within MaskedTextBox. Literals always occupy a static position in the mask at run time and cannot be moved or deleted by the user.

Using the information from Table 3-1, a new mask could be constructed. For example, say that you need a customer number mask that starts with a pound sign (#) and allows three required digits, then a dash, and then three more required digits. The required mask would be:

```
mtbCustomerNumber.Mask = "\#000-000"
```

There is a backslash (\ ) in front of the pound sign because the pound sign (#) is one of the mask elements.

In this case, because you want to use the # as a literal, you need to precede the # with the \ character. This tells the mask property that the # is really being used as a literal. Figure 3-6 shows a MaskedTextBox with a mask of \#000-000.

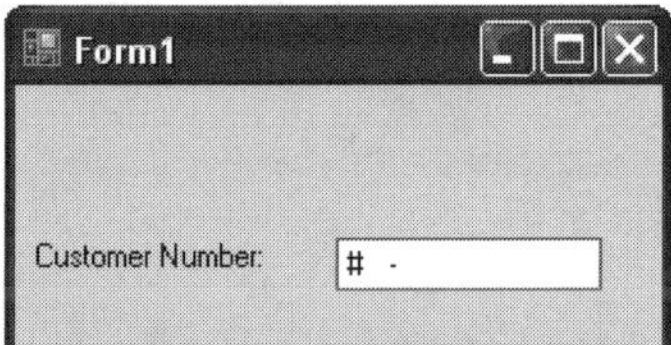

Figure 3-6 MaskedTextBox using a custom Customer number mask

WebBrowser

Imagine you are building an application to maintain a list of books, CDs, or DVDs that you own. You might want your application to display a Web page from Amazon.com that provides additional details about each book, CD, or DVD. The WebBrowser Control allows Web pages to be displayed as part of a Visual Basic Windows Application.

The **WebBrowser** has a number of uses other than just displaying Web pages. Some of the most useful capabilities of the WebBrowser are its ability to print Web pages and save Web pages to a file.

The best way to explore the capabilities of the WebBrowser is to build a simple example named "mini-browser." Mini-browser will have the ability to browse, print, and save Web pages.

Building the Mini-Browser Example

You will follow a series of simple steps with minimal coding to build the mini-browser application.

1. The first step in this example is to create a new Visual Basic 2005 Windows Application. On the VS.NET 2005 menu bar, click **File**, then click **New**, and then click **Project**. In the dialog box that appears, select **Windows Application** to create the new application.

2. On the VS.NET 2005 menu bar, click **View**, then click **Toolbox**. The Toolbox is displayed. Click the **pushpin** in the upper-right corner of the Toolbox to anchor it in place and make sure the **Common Controls** tab in the Toolbox is expanded. Figure 3-7 shows Visual Studio after these actions are carried out.

Figure 3-7 Viewing the Common Controls section of the Toolbox

3. From the Toolbox, drag a **TextBox**, **three buttons**, and a **WebBrowser** onto the form and align them as shown in Figure 3-8. You have to make the form a little larger so the buttons fit.
4. Name the TextBox **txtUrl**, then change the text on the buttons to read **Browse**, **Print**, and **Save**. Name the buttons **cmdBrowser**, **cmdPrint**, and **cmdSave**, respectively. Name the WebBrowser **wbSite**. The end result should look like Figure 3-8.
5. Double-click the **Browse** button and add the following code to the button's event handler:

```
If NOT String.IsNullOrEmpty(txtUrl.Text) Then
  wbSite.Navigate(txtUrl.Text)
End If
```

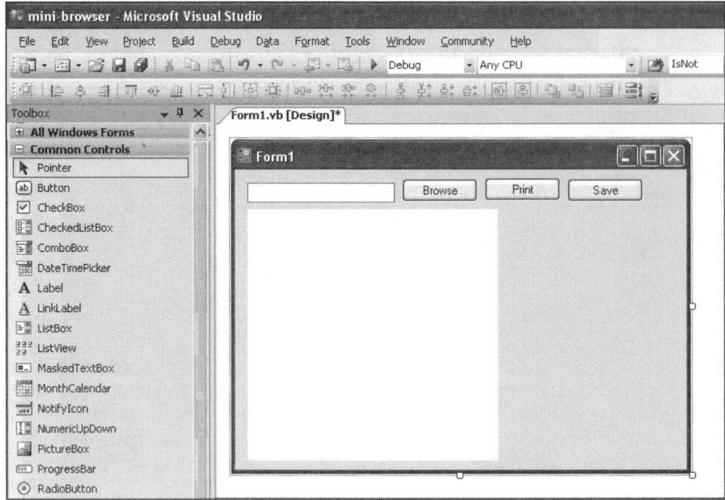

Figure 3-8 Basic mini-browser user interface

The new method in the String class named IsNullOrEmpty allows you to easily check if a string is null or empty.

6. Double-click the **Print** button and add the following code to open the standard Windows print dialog box:

```
wbSite.ShowPrintDialog()
```

7. Double-click the **Save** button and add the following code to open the standard Windows File Save dialog box:

```
wbSite.ShowSaveAsDialog()
```

8. Test the application by pressing **F5** to start the application, typing **www.martinschray.com** in the Textbox, and clicking the **Browse** button.

Congratulations, you have just built a functional browser application.

AutoComplete

The **AutoComplete** feature is not a new control but a capability that has been added to several controls that accept text. The TextBox, ComboBox, ToolStripComboBox, and ToolStripTextBox all provide access to the AutoComplete feature. For example, TextBox controls now have the capability to emulate the behavior of Microsoft Internet Explorer by automatically completing URLs. Figure 3-9 illustrates AutoComplete works for URLs, files in the file system, and directories in the file system.

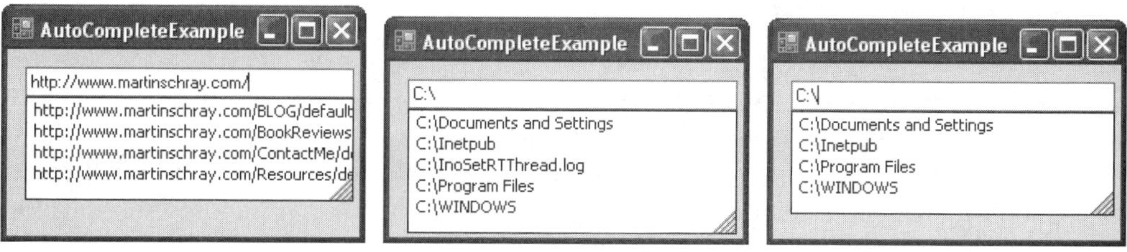

Figure 3-9 TextBox with AutoComplete examples

There are three properties that allow you to configure the operation of AutoComplete: AutoCompleteCollection, AutoCompleteMode, and AutoCompleteSource. There are three modes for AutoCompleteMode, which are Append, Suggest, and SuggestAppend. Append causes the most likely match to be appended to your current data. Suggest mode provides a drop-down list with likely matches. SuggestAppend mode combines the behavior of Suggest and Append. The examples in Figure 3-9 use SuggestAppend for their AutoCompleteMode.

There are a number of AutoComplete sources available as well. The example in Figure 3-9 uses AllUrl, FileSystem, and FileSystemDirectory respectively as the AutoCompleteSource.

A list of AutoCompleteSources can be found in Table 3-2.

Table 3-2 AutoCompleteSources

AutoCompleteSource	Description
AllSystemSources	Specifies a combination of FileSystem and AllUrl as the source for the AutoComplete feature
AllUrl	Specifies a combination of HistoryList and Recently-UsedList as the source for the AutoComplete feature
CustomSource	Specifies that the AutoCompleteStringCollection is the source of the AutoComplete list
FileSystem	Specifies the file system as the source
FileSystemDirectories	Specifies that only directory names and not filenames are automatically completed
HistoryList	Includes the Uniform Resource Locators (URLs) in the Internet Explorer history list
ListItems	Specifies the items from a list, such as a ComboBox, as source
None	Specifies that no AutoCompleteSource is in use; this is the default value of AutoCompleteSource.
RecentlyUsedList	Includes the Uniform Resource Locators (URLs) in the list of those URLs most recently used

New Containers

Have you ever designed a form and thought the layout looks just right? Then you decide to maximize your form and discover that doing so causes all the controls to move to the upper-left corner. Then you reduce the size of your form only to find that the controls are no longer visible. Figures 3-10 and 3-11 illustrate the mini-browser developed in the previous example showing both of these behaviors.

Although **containers** are not as exciting to talk about, as designers they are very useful and can be used to solve a number of application problems. In fact, containers allow both of the resizing problems illustrated in Figures 3-10 and 3-11 to be addressed. A container is simply a control that can contain other controls. This section covers the three new containers in Visual Basic 2005: FlowLayoutPanel, TableLayoutPanel, and SplitContainer. Each container has different properties and can solve different problems. Containers can be found in the container tab of the Toolbox.

Figure 3-10 Mini-browser doesn't handle maximize too well

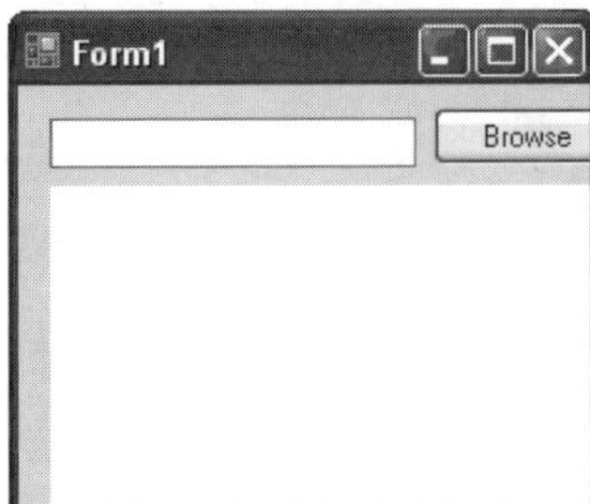

Figure 3-11 Mini-browser doesn't gracefully resize

FlowLayoutPanel

The **FlowLayoutPanel** dynamically lays out the controls it contains, as shown in Figure 3-12. If there is enough space, all the controls flow from left to right. As the amount of horizontal space available becomes smaller and does not support all of the controls, they are stacked vertically.

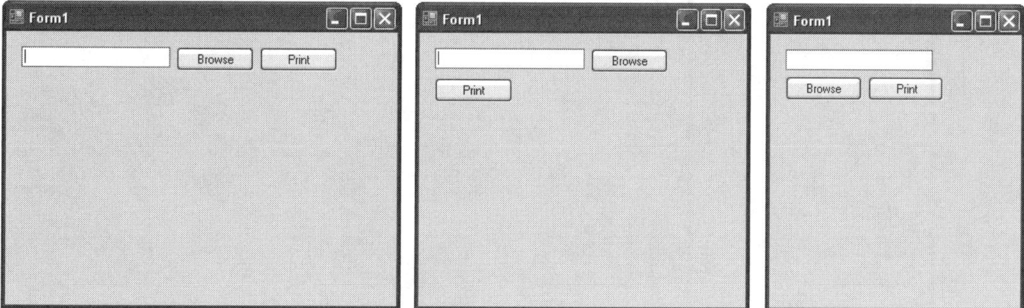

Figure 3-12 FlowLayoutPanel in action

You could have placed the TextBox and Button controls in the mini-browser application in a FlowLayoutPanel to make the browser handle resizing more gracefully. To do so, it is necessary to anchor the FlowLayoutPanel to the form, so that the FlowLayoutPanel expands and contracts with the form. As Figure 3-13 shows, this can be accomplished by accessing the FlowLayoutPanel anchor property. In Figure 3-12 the FlowLayoutPanel is anchored to the left, top, and right. The FlowLayoutPanel is capable of containing multiple controls.

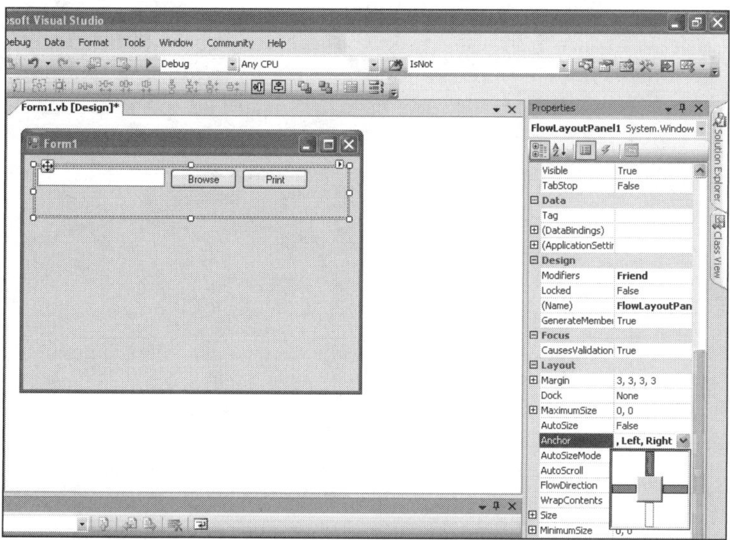

Figure 3-13 Anchoring the FlowLayoutPanel to the form's left, right, and top

The FlowLayoutPanel also provides an AutoScroll property, which defaults to false. When AutoScroll is set to true, scrollbars automatically appear if the space becomes too small to display the controls, as illustrated in Figure 3-14.

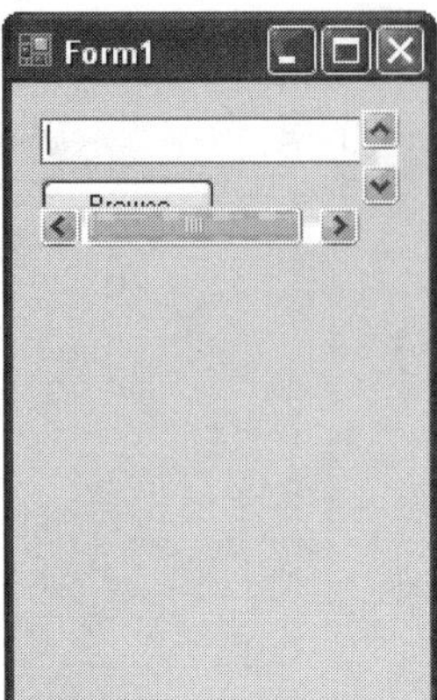

Figure 3-14 Much improved resize behavior with FlowLayoutPanel

The FlowLayoutPanel can layout controls based on the value of the FlowDirection property, with the default being LeftToRight. The acceptable values for FlowDirection are listed in Table 3-3. Figure 3-15 shows the effect of the various flow direction settings.

Table 3-3 Directions that FlowLayoutPanel supports

Flow direction	Description
BottomUp	Elements flow from the bottom of the design surface to the top
LeftToRight	Elements flow from the left edge of the design surface to the right
RightToLeft	Elements flow from the right edge of the design surface to the left
TopDown	Elements flow from the top of the design surface to the bottom

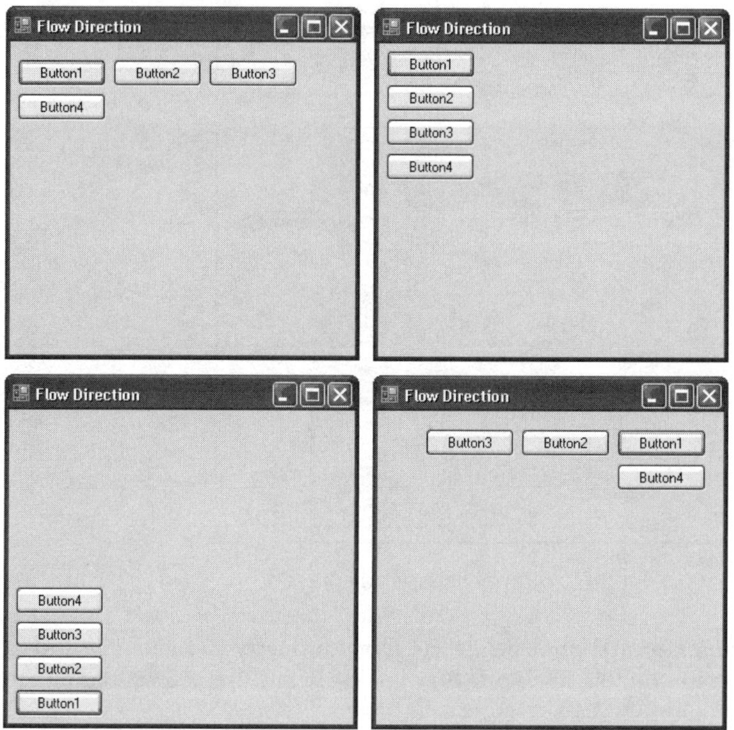

Figure 3-15 FlowLayoutPanel control displaying the four flow direction settings: LeftToRight, TopDown, BottomUp, and RightToLeft

TableLayoutPanel

TableLayoutPanels are meant to provide Windows applications with the table layout capabilities of HTML tables. HTML tables are popular because they allow the space on a Web page to be broken up into rows and columns. Rows and columns can be assigned fixed sizes, or they can fill a percentage of an entire page. This is another time when an example is worth a hundred words.

In the mini-browser application it would make sense if enough space was allocated for the textbox and buttons, and the rest of the page was filled with the browser. Even if the page resized, the space of the textbox and buttons should be maintained, and the browser should fill whatever space is left. Using the FlowLayoutPanel and TableLayoutPanel, this can easily be constructed. Here are the steps to follow:

1. Drag a **TableLayoutPanel** to an empty form. Figure 3-16 shows the form after the drag operation is complete.
2. Click the small **green arrow** in the upper-right corner of the TableLayoutPanel.
3. Click **Remove last column**. This provides a table with one column and two rows.

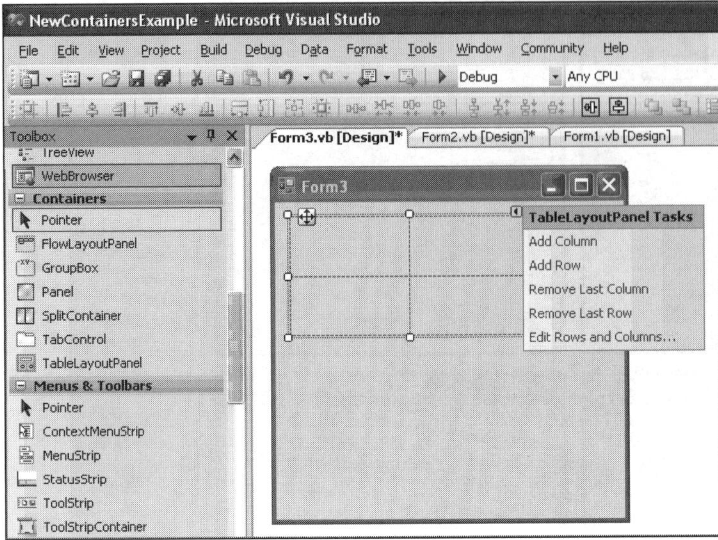

Figure 3-16 Form with TableFlowPanel task list displayed

4. Select the **TableLayoutPanel**. Select the Dock property and click the **Fill** icon. The large square in the middle dock property in Figure 3-17 represents the fill selection.

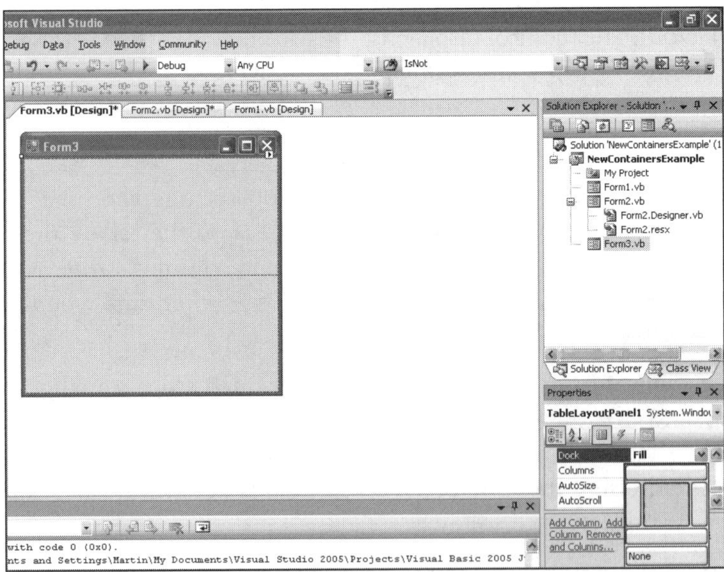

Figure 3-17 Setting TableLayoutPanel's Dock property to fill mode

5. Drag a **FlowLayoutPanel** into the top row of the table.
6. Select the **FlowLayoutPanel**. Using its Anchor property, anchor it to the top, bottom, left, and right.

7. Drag a **TextBox** control and two buttons into the FlowLayoutPanel, as shown in Figure 3-18.

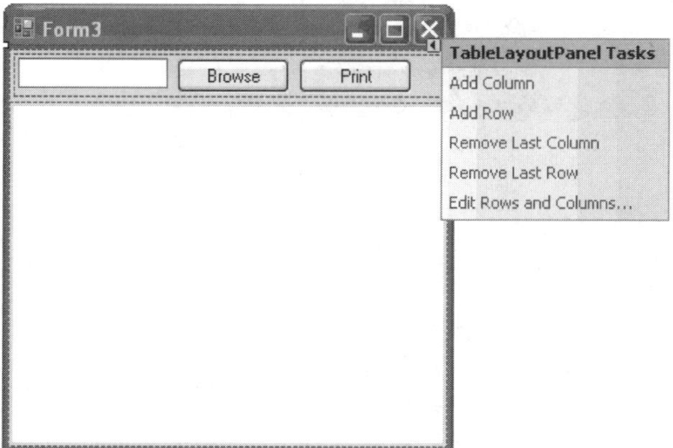

Figure 3-18 Mini-browser user interface revisited

8. Select the **TableLayoutPanel**. Click the small **green arrow** in the upper-right corner of the TableLayoutPanel. Select **Edit Rows and Columns**. The dialog box in Figure 3-19 opens. Select **Rows** from the drop-down list and set the height of Row1 to **35** pixels and the percentage of Row2 to **100**. This causes the first row to have constant height and the second row to fill whatever space is left.

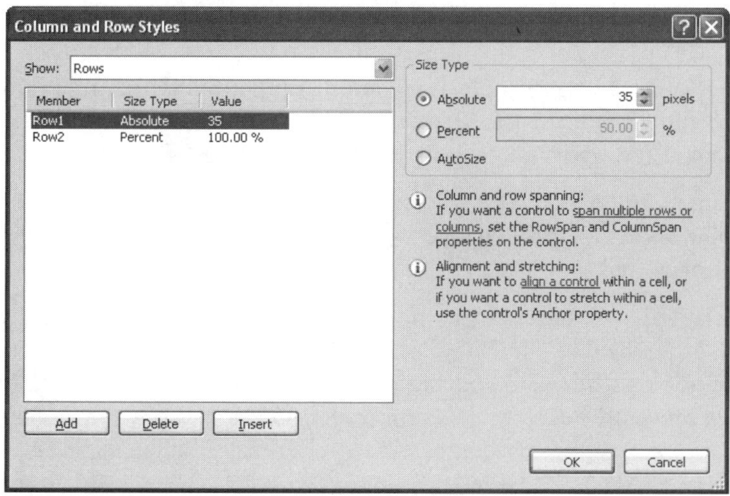

Figure 3-19 Setting the rows' sizing

9. Run it and resize the application to see how it responds, as illustrated in Figure 3-20.

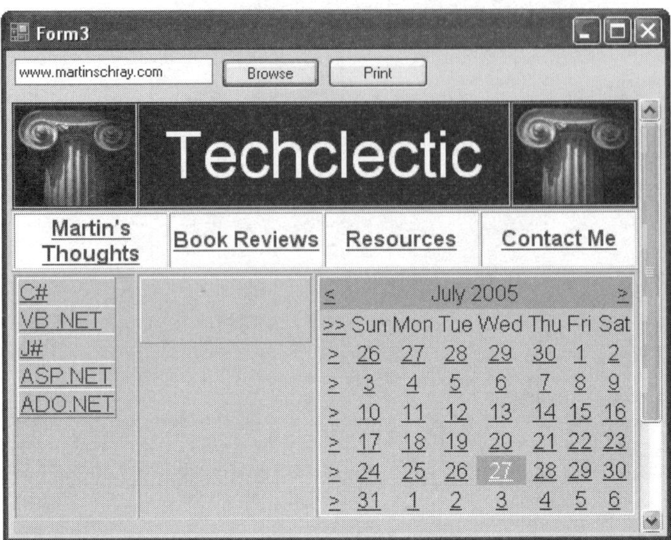

Figure 3-20 Mini-browser with resizing support

SplitContainer

The **SplitContainer** is another container that can be used to construct sophisticated user interfaces for your applications. The SplitContainer is unique in that it contains two panels that are divided by a slider (see Figure 3-21). The developer can place controls on both panels, and the user can use the slider between the panels to give more space to one of the panels.

The images in Figure 3-22 show a simple application using a SplitContainer and how the slider can be used to increase the space between panels. The Split Container defaults to a vertical split, but it can also support a horizontal split, as the images in Figure 3-23 illustrate.

In Figure 3-24, the small green arrow on the top right of the SplitContainer can be clicked to access a menu that allows you to change the orientation of the split from vertical to horizontal or from horizontal to vertical.

In this example there are two buttons in one half of the SplitContainer, and there is a WebControl in the other half of the SplitContainer. The button labeled Microsoft.com directs the WebBrowser to *www.microsoft.com*, and the button labeled MSDN directs the browser to *www.msdn.com*. Although this is a simple example, it lays out the basic uses of the SplitControl.

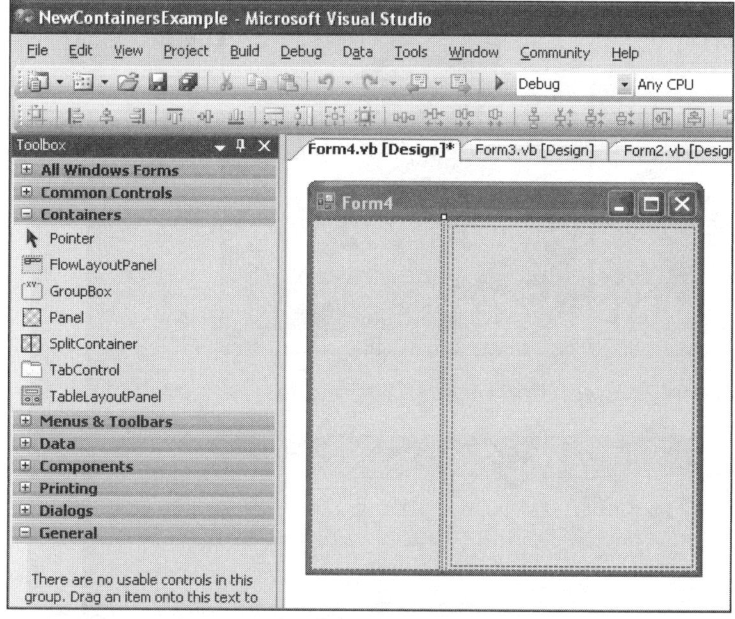

Figure 3-21 SplitContainer on a form

Figure 3-22 Vertical configuration of the SplitContainer

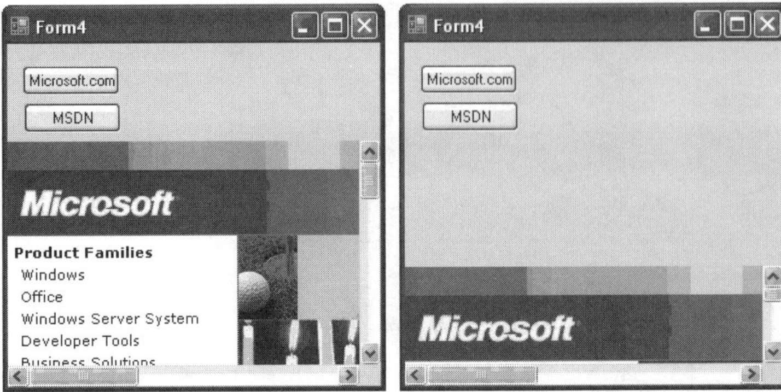

Figure 3-23 Horizontal configuration of the SplitContainer

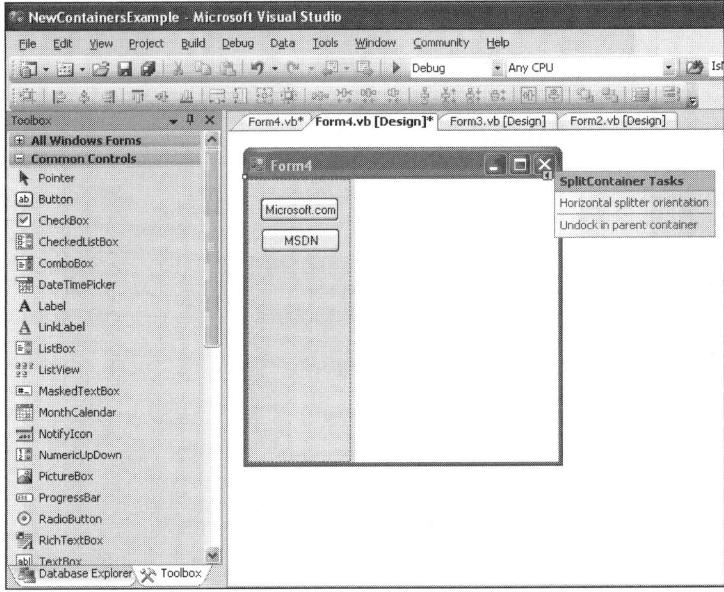

Figure 3-24 SplitContainer with controls placed

Margins and Padding

Containers have a property named **Padding** that allows the developer to specify the amount of space between a container's edge and the control it contains. Padding can be set for a container's left, right, top, and bottom edges. The left image in Figure 3-25 illustrates two TextBox controls in a FlowLayoutPanel with its Padding property set to 0. The right image illustrates the same controls when the FlowLayoutPanel's Padding property is set to 20 for all edges.

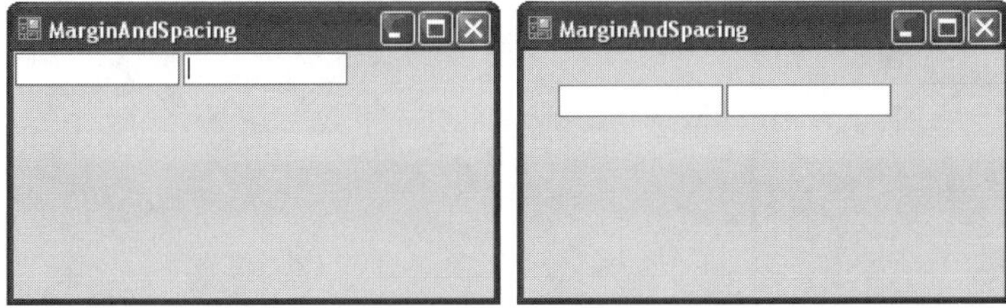

Figure 3-25 FlowLayoutPanel with different padding settings

All visual controls (any control visible on a form) have a Margin property that affects the control's appearance when the control is placed in a container. Margin is the amount of space between the control and its neighboring controls and the container. Margins can be specified for the top, bottom, left, and right of a control. The left image in Figure 3-26 shows two TextBox controls with their Margin property set to 1. The right image in Figure 3-26 shows the same TextBox controls, but each now has its Margin property set to 20. Note the space around and in between the TextBox controls. What is the difference between padding and margins? Padding affects the space between the container and the controls it contains. Margin is the space around a control in a container.

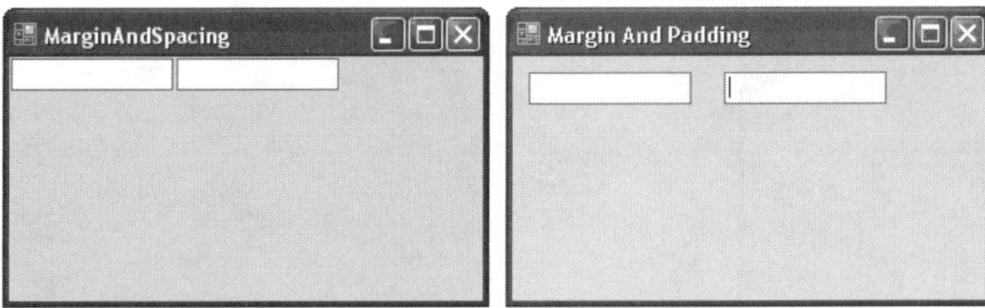

Figure 3-26 Two TextBox controls with different margin settings

New Menus and Toolbars

The menus and toolbars in Microsoft Office 2003 offer many helpful features and uses. There were a number of requests for Visual Basic 2005 to pick up some of the sophisticated menu and toolbar capabilities of Microsoft Office. As a result, there are some pretty substantial enhancements to menus and toolbars in Visual Basic 2005.

Menus are now called MenuStrips and now support TextBox controls and ComboBox controls as part of the menu. Figure 3-27 and Figure 3-28 show a menu with a ComboBox and TextBox. The name of the class that supports a MenuStrip or ToolStrip ComboBox is ToolStripComboBox. The name of the class that supports a MenuStrip or ToolStrip TextBox is ToolStripTextBox.

In Visual Basic .NET 2003, only MenuItem and Separator were supported in a menu, which was pretty boring. As Figure 3-31 illustrates, MenuStrips in Visual Basic 2005 support MenuItem, Separator, ToolStripComboBox, and ToolStripTextBox.

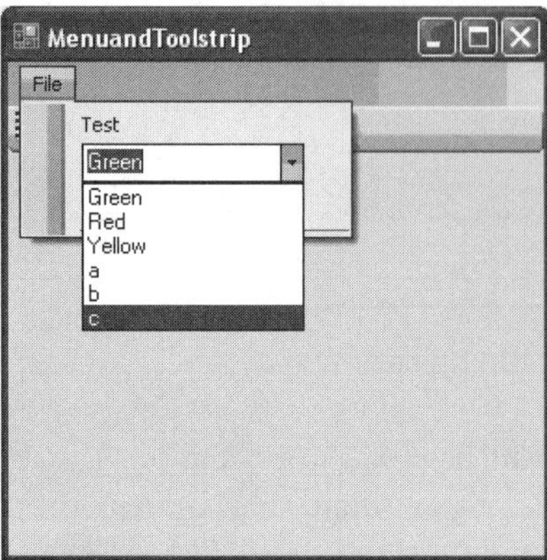

Figure 3-27 Menu with ToolStripComboBox

Figure 3-28 Menu with ToolStripTextBox

Toolbars in Visual Basic 2005 are now referred to as ToolStrips. ToolStrips allow developers to build toolbars that make it easy for users to interact with applications. ToolStrips make it easy for a user to access functionality in a common location (ToolStrip) that can be used through the entire application. ToolStrips have an incredible amount of flexibility and can use the following controls:

- ToolStripButton
- ToolStripLabel
- ToolStripSplitButton
- ToolStripDropDownButton
- ToolStripSeparator
- ToolStripComboBox
- ToolStripTextBox
- ToolStripProgressBar

Figure 3-29 shows a menu item being added to the MenuStrip. The result of adding an item from this list to a ToolStrip is shown in Figure 3-30.

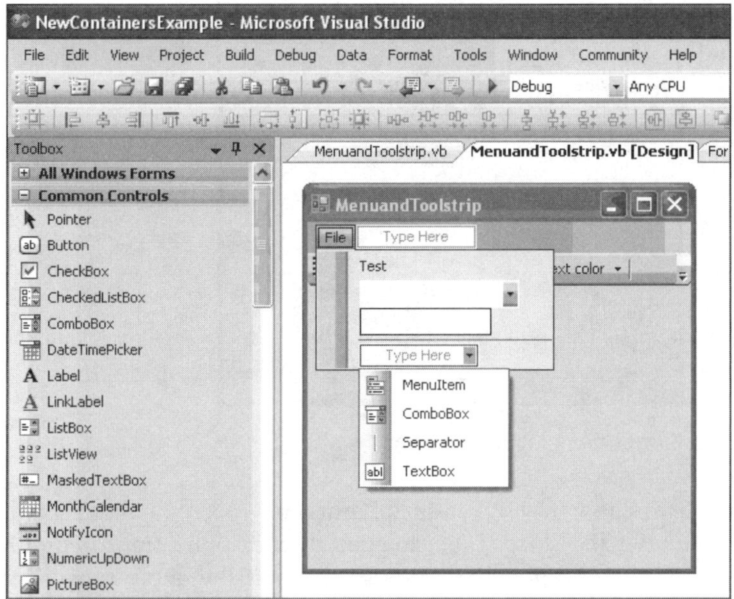

Figure 3-29 Adding an item to a MenuStrip

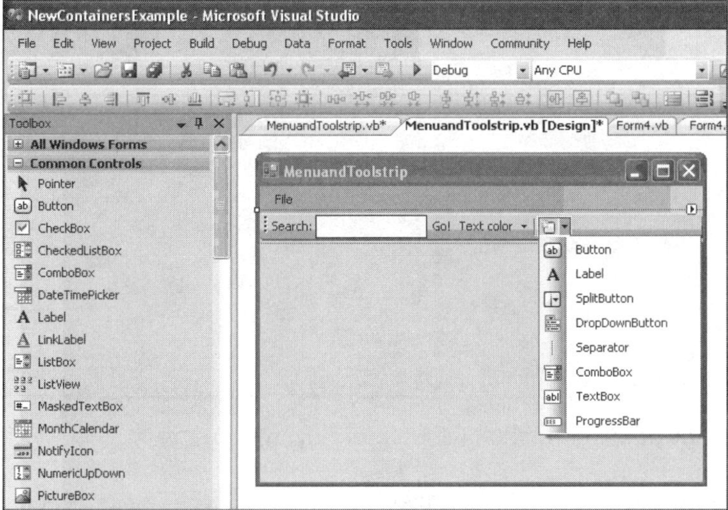

Figure 3-30 Adding an item to a ToolStrip

As Figure 3-31 illustrates there is also a ToolStripContainer. The ToolStripContainer is a container for ToolStrips. The reason for having a ToolStripContainer is to allow ToolStrips to be moved and anchored to the top, bottom, left, or right of a form.

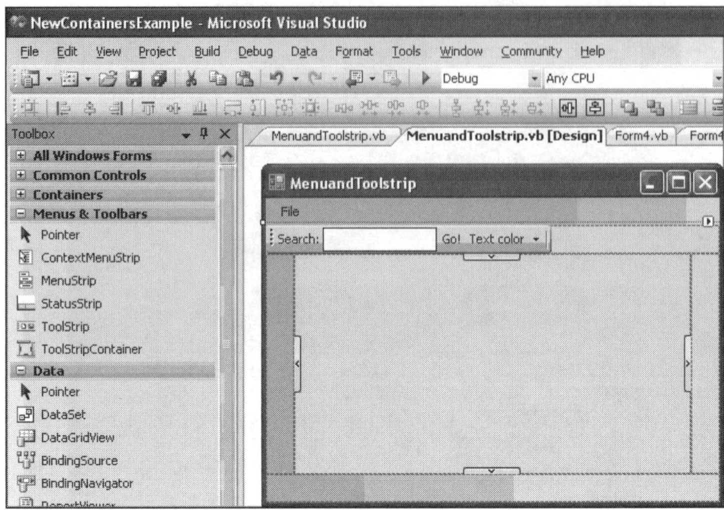

Figure 3-31 ToolStripContainer placed on form

Figure 3-32 shows a form that has a ToolStripContainer that contains a ToolStrip. The ToolStripContainer allows a ToolStrip to be dragged by the application user and anchored to the top or bottom or left or right sides of a form when the application is running. A ToolStripContainer also allows a developer to configure where the ToolStrip can be anchored by the user when the application is running (Figure 3-33).

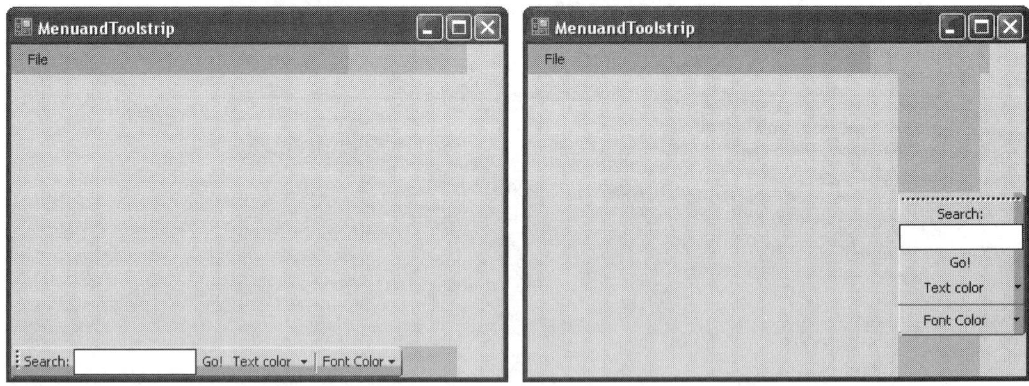

Figure 3-32 ToolStripContainer enabling ToolStrip movement

A highly functional version of the mini-browser application can be built using a ToolStrip control and its supporting controls. The revised version of the mini-browser application can be seen in Figure 3-34. The revised version of this application contains a ToolStripContainer, ToolStrip, ToolStripLabel, ToolStripTextBox, two ToolStripButtons, and WebBrowser controls. It provides similar functionality to the previous versions of the application, while providing the ability to move the ToolStrip to any side of the application by simply dragging it to the desired location. In addition, the ToolStripTextBox has been configured to use AutoComplete by setting its AutoCompleteMode to AppendSuggest and its AutoCompleteSource to AllUrl. The code for the Browse and Print buttons are identical to the original mini-browser example.

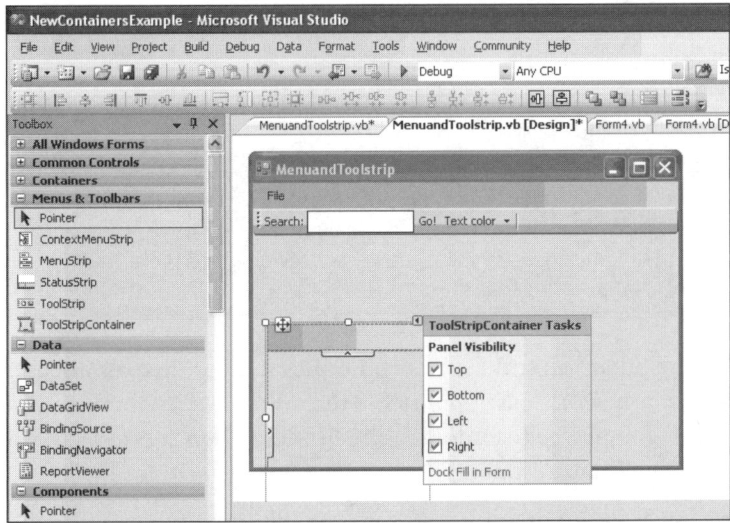

Figure 3-33 ToolStripContainer allows specification of where ToolStrips can dock

Figure 3-34 ToolStrip version of mini-browser

New Components

BackgroundWorker and SerialPort are two new components that have been introduced in Visual Basic 2005. **Components** are similar to controls, but they don't actually appear in an application's user interface. Table 3-4 provides a basic description of what each new component actually does.

Table 3-4 New components in Visual Basic 2005

Component	Description
BackgroundWorker	A component that makes it easy to coordinate the operation of code running on different threads
SerialPort	A component that makes it easy to read and write data to a computer's serial ports

The BackgroundWorker builds on some advanced topics such as threads and asynchronous execution. The .NET Framework has support for threading and asynchronous execution. For example, the .NET Framework supports asynchronous Web services, and ADO.NET 2.0 supports asynchronous database operations.

Threads basically let you break your application into small units of work that the processor can schedule and execute. Although you can write code to use multiple threads, once you move beyond a single thread things can get quite complex; at that point ensuring that all the threads work in harmony can be difficult. In general, threading should be avoided without significant knowledge of threading and a compelling reason to use threads. Threaded programming is an advanced topic and won't be covered in more depth here. For additional information search the Visual Studio 2005 online help for "Threading Design Guidelines".

If you build a Visual Basic 2005 application it uses a single thread. There is a rule in Windows Forms programming that says "only update the user interface (UI) from the thread that created the user interface." The BackgroundWorker was developed to safely and easily allow a thread that didn't create the UI to update the UI.

If you need to use asynchronous Web services, or an ADO.NET 2.0 asynchronous database operations, and need to update UI, you should strongly consider using the BackgroundWorker component.

Serial ports have been on personal computers (PCs) since the PC's inception. Serial ports allow data to be read or written to a serial device external to the computer. Serial printers were standard for PCs before parallel and USB printers became popular.

By using the SerialPort component, it is easy to read and write data to serial ports. The following example gathers a list of serial ports from the computer and writes the list out to the console. Next the code opens the serial port named COM1, and after making sure it is open, reads data from the serial port. Finally, it writes data to the port and then closes the port.


```
Dim portList() As String = _
            System.IO.Ports.SerialPort.GetPortNames()

        For Each str As String In portList
            Console.WriteLine(str)
        Next

        SerialPort1.PortName = "COM1"
        SerialPort1.Open()

        If SerialPort1.IsOpen() Then

            Dim portData As String = _
                SerialPort1.ReadExisting()

            Console.WriteLine(portData)

            SerialPort1.WriteLine("HelloWorld")

            SerialPort1.Close()
        End If
```

A common use for a serial port is to acquire data from a device such as a Global Position Satellite (GSP) receiver that provides very accurate location information. Another common use for serial ports is to read and write data to **Bluetooth**-enabled devices. Bluetooth is a standard for short-range wireless communication between devices.

Microsoft.com describes Bluetooth as "A wireless technology specification for radio links between mobile computers, mobile phones, and other portable devices. The radio links are small-form factor, low cost, and short range."

Many modern devices such as a wireless mouse, wireless keyboards, wireless headsets, and GPS receivers communicate using Bluetooth. Bluetooth devices can be accessed via serial ports. Once a Bluetooth device has been accessed, it can be read from and written to just like a standard serial port. With Visual Basic 2005's new support for serial ports, it is easier to connect and receive data from these other devices.

Chapter Summary

This chapter provided details about the new capabilities of Visual Basic 2005 for building Windows applications.

- The MaskedTextBox provides visual clues to the user for the type of data that should be entered. Validation rules make sure only valid data can be entered.
- The WebControl is a very powerful browser that allows Web pages to be viewed, printed, and saved to a file.
- The new containers FlowLayoutPanel, TableLayoutPanel, and SplitContainer make it much easier to build sophisticated user interface applications that are resizable.
- MenuStrips and ToolStrips allow Visual Basic 2005 applications to mimic the menu and toolbar behavior found in Microsoft Office 2003 with menus and an assortment of controls such as ToolStripTextBox and ToolStripComboBox.
- There are new components in Visual Basic 2005 that support reading from serial ports as well other advanced capabilities.

CHAPTER

4

ENHANCEMENTS TO WEB FORMS APPLICATIONS

In this chapter you will:

- Learn about the new file-based ASP.NET projects
- Realize the power to control how pages look with master pages and themes
- Discover how to use the new profile facility to store user information
- Leverage membership, roles, and security controls to allow users to log on to your Web site

This chapter is not meant to serve as an introduction to ASP.NET, but rather is designed for those developers with some level of experience using ASP.NET. There are other excellent Course Technology texts that can serve to introduce ASP.NET development, so this chapter looks at the most compelling new features of ASP.NET 2.0.

ASP.NET 2.0 brings a huge set of new features and capabilities to ASP.NET Web developers. ASP.NET 2.0 supports a file-based Web project that removes the requirement for Internet Information Server (IIS) and FrontPage Server Extensions to allow Web applications to be developed and tested. For academic and hobbyist developers, this makes it much easier to start developing Web projects and removes many of the configuration hassles found in Visual Studio .NET 2002 and 2003.

ASP.NET 2.0 includes two new features named master pages and themes that allow you to provide a standard look and feel for your application. Master pages allow you to build a template page that has layout elements such as headers, footers, and basic navigation. You can then apply this master page to other pages on the site to provide a standard look and feel for these pages. Themes are a combination of Cascading Style Sheets (CSS), images, and skin files that allow pages and ASP.NET server controls to have a standard appearance. Themes allow for fonts, colors, and images to be specified, thus allowing a site to have a standard visual look and feel.

ASP.NET also provides the ability to easily save user information through a new capability named Profiles. Profiles make it easy to store information such as a user's zip code, birthday, or phone number as part of your ASP.NET application. Profiles are a huge improvement over using cookies or session variables for storing this type of information.

Finally, ASP.NET provides authentication and authorization facilities to allow users to log on to Web applications and to be assigned security roles. These authentication and authorization features also provide new security controls that make logging on and off a Web application safer and easier, as well as facilitating support-related activities such as password reminders and the ability to change passwords.

Projects No Longer Require IIS

Historically, creating Web projects in Visual Studio .NET 2002 and 2003 had some significant configuration requirements and a number of shortcomings. Visual Studio .NET 2002 and 2003 required Internet Information Server to be available to develop Web projects. IIS needed FrontPage Server Extensions installed to allow Visual Studio .NET 2002 and 2003 to communicate with it. Additionally, Web projects had to have special directories called **Virtual Directories (vdirs)** that were created and maintained by IIS. Furthermore, only a single user at a time could debug Web applications using the Visual Studio .NET 2002 and 2003 debugger. Finally, to debug Web applications a user had to have administrator privileges, which in academic settings was often problematic.

All in all, this made creating, developing, debugging, and maintaining Web projects much harder than standard Windows Forms projects. This also meant that a fair amount of software had to be installed and configured before a Web project could be started. All other project types in Visual Studio .NET 2002 and 2003 simply created projects directly in the file system.

For professional developers, having IIS is usually not an issue, but for hobbyist and academics it can be. ASP.NET 2.0 introduces a new file-based Web project that doesn't require IIS or FrontPage Server Extensions. Additionally, using the file-based approach also removes the requirements for administrative privileges to debug Web applications.

Visual Basic 2005 greatly simplifies Web project creation by removing the requirement for IIS, FrontPage Server Extensions, and virtual directories. In Visual Basic 2005 Web projects are file based. This simply means all files for the project exist in the file system and don't require IIS, FrontPage Server Extensions, and virtual directories to allow editing of the files. A Web server is still needed to host a Web site so the ASP.NET Development Web Server is provided in Visual Studio 2005. ASP.NET Development Web Server is a single-user Web server used to facilitate development and testing. This Web server runs only when Visual Studio 2005 is running, accepts requests only from the system it is running on, and ASP.NET Development Web Server is written entirely in managed code. These three factors make the Web server in Visual Studio 2005 very secure.

Creating Visual Studio 2005 Web projects is a little different than in Visual Studio .NET 2002 and 2003. In Visual Studio .NET 2002 and 2003, all new projects were created by opening the VS .NET 2003 menu, and then clicking File and New Project. To create a new Web project in Visual Studio 2005, click File, New, then click Web Site. This opens the New Web Site dialog box, which you use to create a new Web site project, as illustrated in Figure 4-1. By default a file system Web project is created, meaning that IIS and FrontPage Server Extensions are not required. If you want to create a site that uses IIS and FrontPage Server Extensions, just as you did previously in VS .NET 2002 and 2003, click HTTP from the Location list box, as shown in Figure 4-2. The Location list box also offers an FTP (File Transfer Protocol) choice, if you prefer to use FTP to transfer the files in your Web project to your Web server. Whether you choose File System, HTTP, or FTP, the way you develop your Web projects using Visual Studio 2005 hasn't changed.

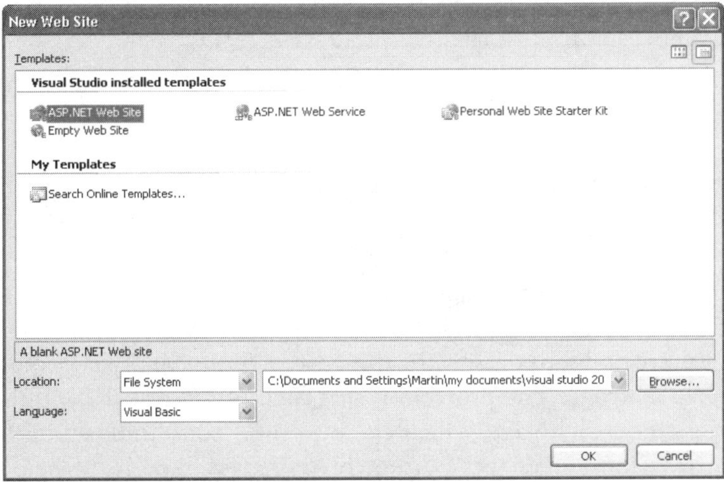

Figure 4-1 New Web Site dialog box using File System

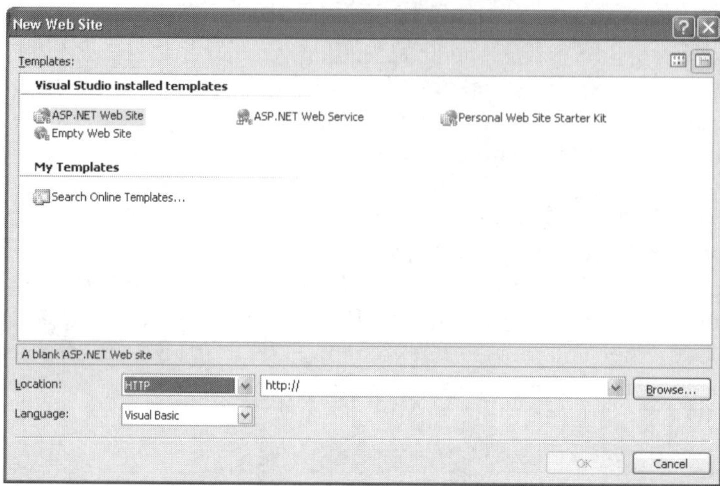

Figure 4-2 Choosing to use IIS and virtual directories like VS .NET 2002 and 2003 used

Master Pages

Most Web sites have a standard template that is followed by almost all pages on a site. For example, almost all pages on a site typically have a standard header, footer, and navigation elements (menu or list of links). Rather than have to re-create this standard look on each page, many developers create user controls for the header, footer, and navigation elements that can be reused on each page. The problem is that each of these user controls must still be placed and positioned on each page, which can be a time-consuming and monotonous task. Visual Studio 2005 introduces the concept of the **master page** to help make the creation of a standardized look and feel for a Web site much easier.

Master pages are template pages in which headers, footers, and navigation elements can be specified. The master page also provides a **content placeholder**. The content placeholder is where the content goes on the standard pages of a Web site that use the master page as a template. The process starts by creating your master page as shown in the following steps.

1. To create a new Web project, click **File**, **New**, and then click **Web Site**. Name the Web site, then click **OK**.
2. To create a master page, click **File** on the VS menu, click **Web site**, then click **Add New Item** to display the Add New Item dialog box. From the list of available templates, select **Master Page**, then click **Add**. A new master page is created and is opened in the source view.
3. On the VS menu, click **View**, then click **Designer** to ensure you are in the Designer view, as shown in Figure 4-3.

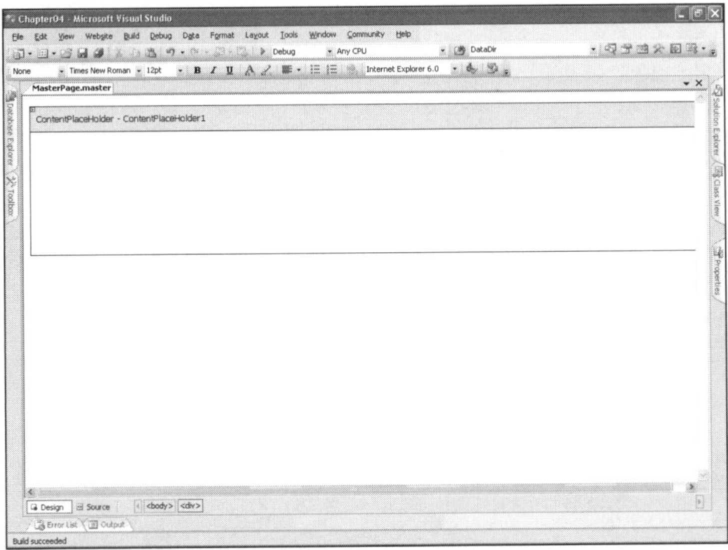

Figure 4-3 The master page in Designer view

4. Next set up the basic page layout by inserting a table. In the VS menu, click **Layout**, then click **Insert Table** to display the Insert Table dialog box. Fill the values in the Insert Table dialog box to match the values in Figure 4-4.

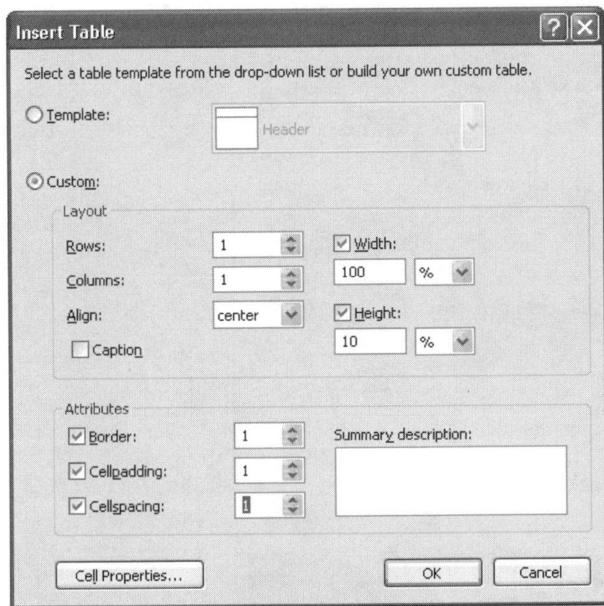

Figure 4-4 Insert Table dialog box

5. Click the **Cell Properties** button on the Insert Table dialog box to open the Cell Properties dialog box. Fill in the fields of the dialog box using the values shown in Figure 4-5, then click **OK** in the Cell Properties and Insert Table dialog boxes.

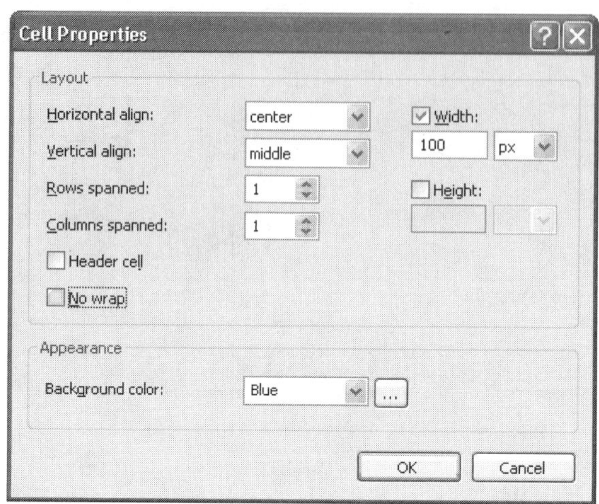

Figure 4-5 Cell Properties dialog box

6. Click in the center of the new table you just created. On the VS menu, click **Format**, then click **Style** to open the Style Builder dialog box, as shown in Figure 4-6. Fill in the values as shown in Figure 4-6, then click **OK**.

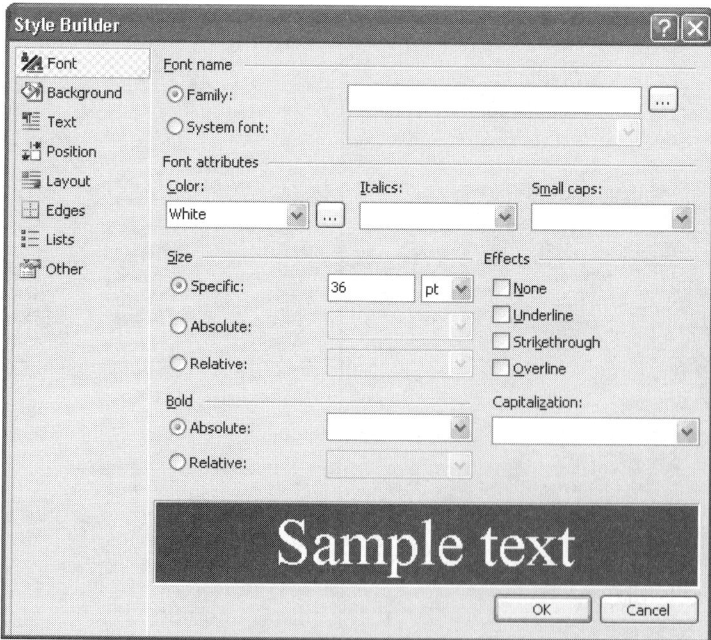

Figure 4-6 Style Builder dialog box

7. Type **Test Site**.

Your master page is now created, as shown in Figure 4-7. The next step is to create a content page that uses the master page as a template.

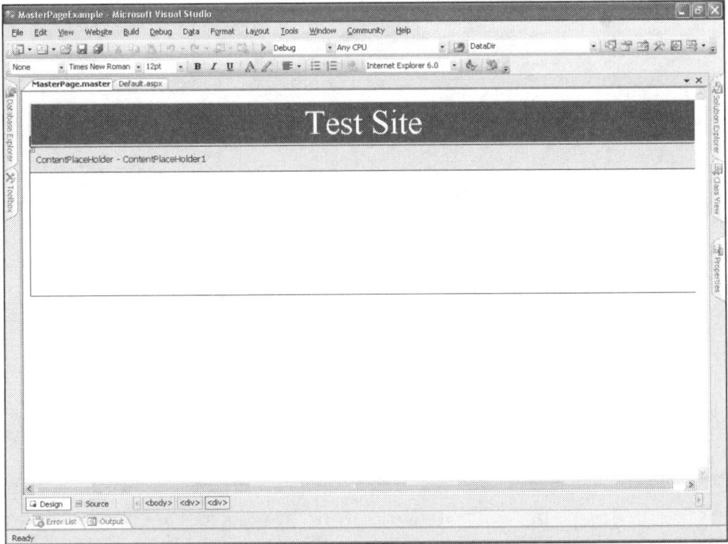

Figure 4-7 The completed master page

1. To create a new content Web page, click **Website** on the VS menu, then click **Add New Item**. The dialog box shown in Figure 4-8 opens to allow the type of new item to be selected.

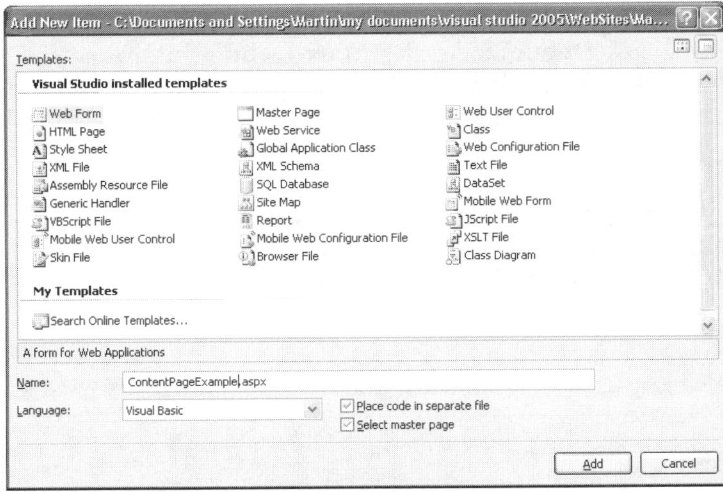

Figure 4-8 The Add New Item dialog box

2. Click **Web Form** and make sure the **Select master page** check box is checked. Click **Add**. The **Select a Master Page** dialog box opens, as shown in Figure 4-9. Click **MasterPage.master**, then click **OK**. This allows a master page to be selected for the new content page.

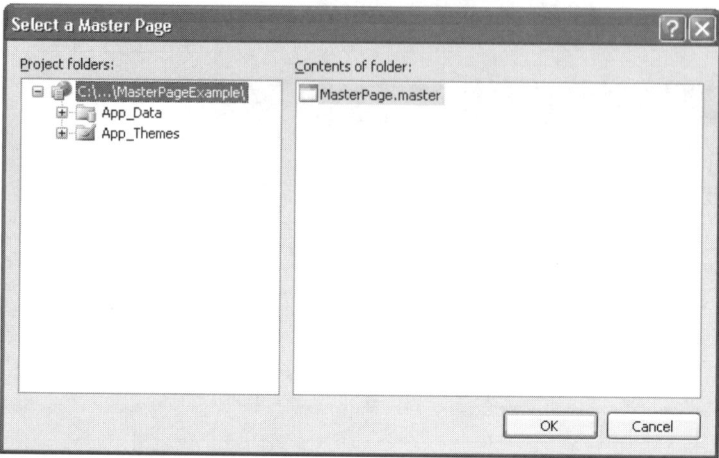

Figure 4-9 Selecting a master page for a new content page

3. On the VS menu, click **Website** and then click **Set As Startup Page**. This makes this page the new default page when you run the application.
4. From the VS menu, click **View**, then click **Designer**; this ensures that you are in the Designer view for the new Web form.
5. Click and drag a TextBox control and a Button control from the Toolbox and place them on to the form, as illustrated in Figure 4-10.
6. On the VS menu, click **Debug**, then click **Start Debugging** to test the application. Figure 4-11 shows how the Web page looks at runtime. When the Web application starts, Visual Studio may offer to create a Web.config file. If it does, click **OK**.

Master pages can be edited and changed, as necessary, and the changes are reflected in all pages using that master page. If necessary you can create and use several different master pages if different sections of your Web site require a different look and feel.

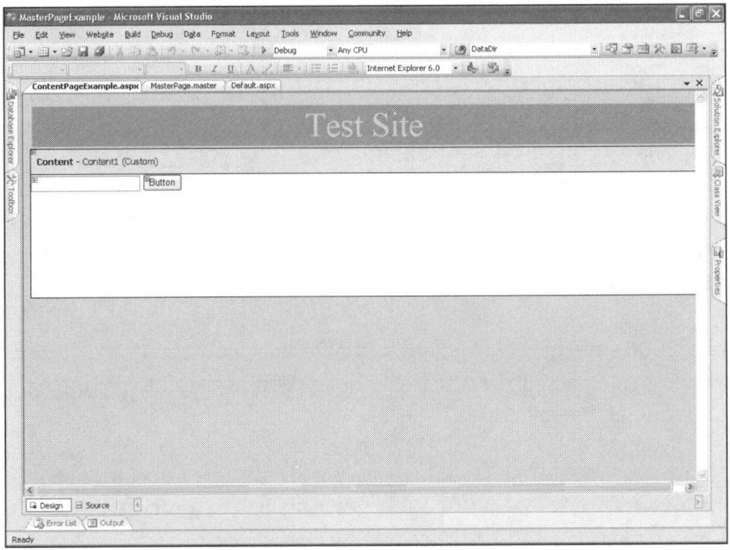

Figure 4-10 New page using master page as a template

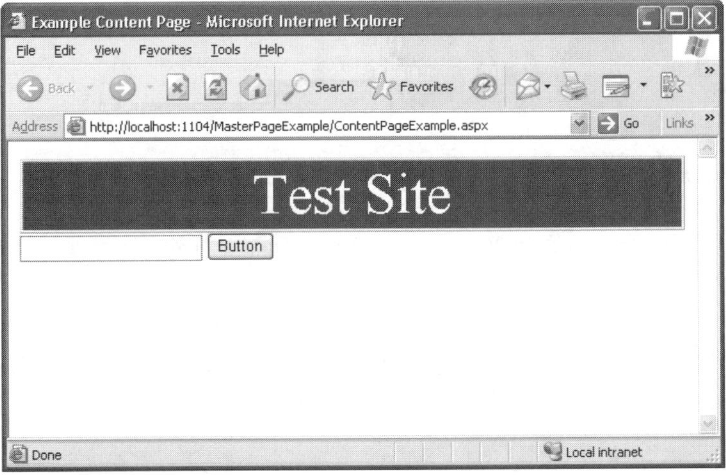

Figure 4-11 Page built using a master page

Themes

ASP.NET 2.0 also adds theme support. Theme support provides a new way to specify the appearance and characteristics of a Web site, Web page, or the server controls on a page. Although a master page is a template for the layout (headers, footers, and basic navigation) of a page, a theme allows you to control the appearance of a page and the appearance of server controls on a page. For example, you could use a theme to ensure that every page on your Web site has a yellow background and each TextBox control on your Web site has a background color of blue and uses the Arial font.

Visual Studio 2005's online help defines a theme as a collection of control properties, style sheets, and images that can be applied as a unit to a page or Web site to define an overall appearance.

A theme is a combination of Cascading Style Sheets (CSS), skin files, and images for use in the theme. A **theme** resides in a folder on your Web site; this folder contains a Cascading Style Sheet (CSS), images, and a **skin** file. Cascading Style Sheets are beyond the scope of this book, but basically they can allow you to define fonts and colors and other similar attributes for HTML pages. Although CSSs are powerful, they have limited capabilities for sophisticated controls such as the GridView, which is where the theme skin file can help.

You will hear the term *skinning* used to define the process of building and applying a theme to a site. You will also hear the term *skins* used when themes are being discussed. Skin files allow the look and feel of server controls to be specified.

A Web site can have a number of themes each with its own folder containing Cascading Style Sheets, images, and a skin file. Themes can be applied to entire applications (using the web.config file), a page (using the @page directive), or specific controls on a page. Here are the steps required to create a new theme.

1. A theme can be created from the VS menu by clicking **View**, then clicking **Solution Explorer**.
2. From Solution Explorer, right-click the project, click **Add Folder**, and then click **Theme Folder**.
3. Right-click the new theme folder that was created, then click **Add New Item**. The Add New Item dialog box will be displayed similarly to Figure 4-12.
4. Click **Skin File**, then click **Add**. This causes Visual Studio 2005 to place the new skin file in the selected theme folder, as shown in Figure 4-13.

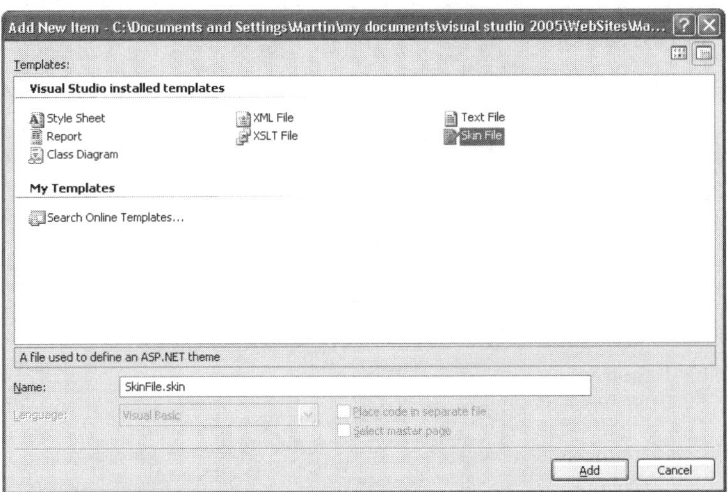

Figure 4-12 Skin File selected

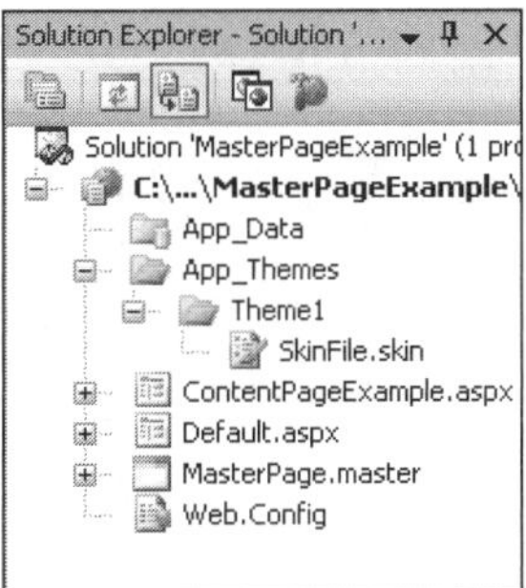

Figure 4-13 Theme folders

A theme can also be assigned to a page by opening the page's Properties dialog box and setting the page's Theme property. A list of valid themes are available in the list box to select from, as illustrated in Figure 4-14.

There are times when you may not want certain controls to be affected by themes. Setting a control's EnableTheming to "false" ensures a control is not affected by themes. In Figure 4-15 the two labels just below the page header (Test Site) have their theme support disabled. Pages can also have their theme disabled by adding EnableTheming="false" to a page's @page directive.

The following declarations are in Theme1's skin file. The first line states that any TextBox control that has its SkinId set equal to *test* gets a BackColor of blue. The second line

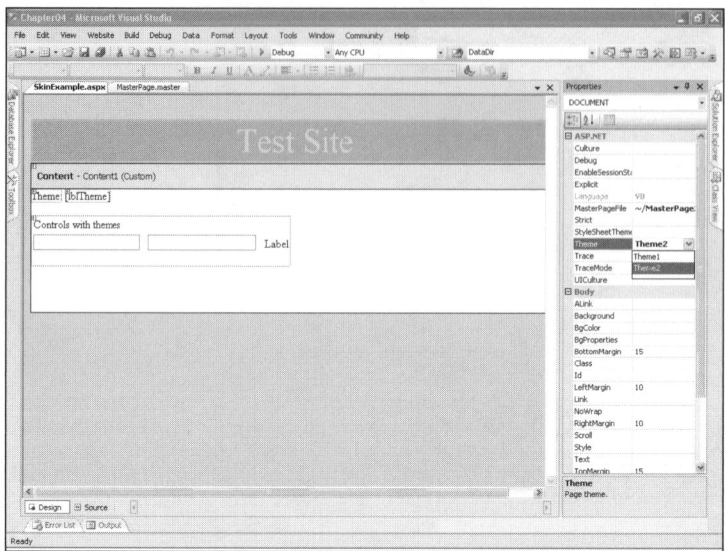

Figure 4-14 Assigning a theme to a page

indicates that TextBox controls use the Webdings font. The third line indicates that Label controls all have a background color of gray and a border. Figure 4-15 shows a page using Theme1.

```
<asp:TextBox SkinId="test" runat="server"  BackColor="Blue" />
<asp:TextBox runat="server" Font-Names="Webdings" />
<asp:Label runat="server" BackColor="gray"
BorderStyle="Solid"></asp:Label>
```

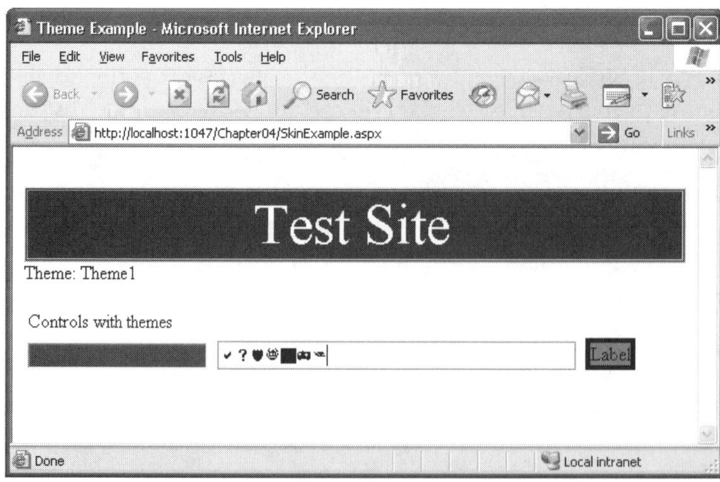

Figure 4-15 Page using Theme1

Following the steps outlined previously, a second theme can be defined. The following declarations are in the Theme2 skin file. The first line states that any TextBox control that has a SkinId equal to *test* gets a BackColor of pink. The second line indicates that TextBox controls use the Webdings font. The third line indicates that Label controls all have a background color of red and a border. Figure 4-16 shows a page using Theme2.


```
<asp:TextBox SkinId="test" runat="server"  BackColor="pink" />
<asp:TextBox runat="server" Font-Names="Webdings" />
<asp:Label runat="server" BackColor="red"
BorderStyle="Solid"></asp:Label>
```

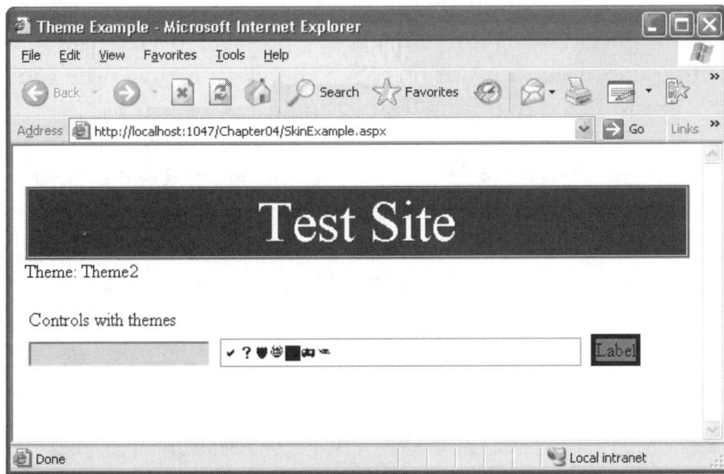

Figure 4-16 Page using Theme2

Themes provide sophisticated capabilities for controlling many characteristics of Web pages as well as the server controls displayed on a page.

Profiles

Have you ever wanted to permanently store information about a user of your Web site? Perhaps a birthday, a color preference, or an e-mail address? There are a couple of ways of accomplishing this, such as storing the information in a **cookie**, or writing a fair amount of code to store this information in a file or database for each user.

A cookie is a file that is stored on the user's hard drive by the Web browser.

There are pieces of data such as credit card numbers, Social Security numbers, and other personal data that should not be stored in cookies. Cookies are just text files on the user's machine, and storing that type of data in a cookie is inappropriate and poses a serious security risk.

Session variables are associated with a user's browser session and last only until the browser is closed, so they are not considered permanent.

As already discussed, it is often necessary to store Profile information about a user, so is there anything in ASP.NET 2.0 and Visual Basic 2005 to make the job of storing this information easier? The answer is a resounding *yes*. Imagine just adding a couple of lines to a configuration file and having the ability to permanently store user information. The new Profile capability in ASP.NET 2.0 provides this ability. Each Web project has a file named web.config that has the entire configuration settings for that Web site. This file is in the root directory of your Web project and can be edited using Visual Studio 2005.

The web.config is just a text file, so it can be edited with any text editor, but it is recommended you edit web.config using Visual Studio (VS) 2005. This is because Intellisense is fully supported when VS 2005 is used to edit the web.config file.

A very simple web.config file is shown in this example:

```
<?xml version="1.0"?>
<configuration
xmlns="http://schemas.microsoft.com/.NetConfiguration/v2.0">
<system.web>
<authorization>
<allow users="mschray" />
</authorization>
<authentication mode="Forms" />
<compilation debug="true"/>
</system.web>
</configuration>
```

By adding the following lines to the web.config file, this application would have two properties associated with the Profile object:

```
<anonymousIdentification enabled="true" />
<profile>
<properties>
<add name="City"
type="System.String" allowAnonymous="true" />
<add name="State"
type="System.String" allowAnonymous="true"/>
</properties>
</profile>
```

After adding these lines to the web.config file, the City and State information can be easily captured and permanently stored and retrieved in code for each Web site user. The part of the declaration that looks like allowAnonymous="true" allows information to be stored for a user that has not logged on yet. If you remove this part of the declaration, the user will need to be logged on before properties can be accessed.

The revised web.config file with the Profile configuration for City and State added and shown in bold follows:

```
<?xml version="1.0"?>
<configuration xmlns="http://schemas.microsoft.com/.
NetConfiguration/v2.0">
<system.web>
<anonymousIdentification enabled="true" />
<profile>
<properties>
<add name="City"
type="System.String" allowAnonymous="true" />
<add name="State"
type="System.String" allowAnonymous="true"/>
</properties>
</profile>

<authorization>
<allow users="mschray" />
</authorization>
<authentication mode="Forms" />
<compilation debug="true"/>
</system.web>
</configuration>
```

Once the configuration information for City and State is added to the web.config file you can use these Profile properties in your application, as the following example illustrates. The following code shows the use of the Profile variables City and State. The code first checks to see if this page is being rendered for the first time, using Page.IsPostBack. If it is not a postback, then the page is initially being rendered to the browser. The values are retrieved by the profile for this particular user and displayed in two text boxes. If this page is being posted back, then the values are pulled out of TextBox controls and assigned to the Profile object, and the Profile object' Save method is called to save this information to the profile for this user:

```
        If (Not Page.IsPostBack) Then
            txtCity.Text = Profile.City
            txtState.Text = Profile.State
        Else
            Profile.City = txtCity.Text
            Profile.State = txtState.Text

            ' save the profile
            Profile.Save()
        End If
    End Sub
```

Membership, Roles, and Security Controls (Oh My)

Membership, **roles**, and **security controls** are all related to each other. Membership is the ability to define users of a Web site, as when you want to define a small group of your friends who can access the information on your site.

Roles offer the ability to indicate that certain users can perform actions on the site and others can't. Based on the users you set up in the memberships system, you can assign users different roles. For example, maybe you allow certain of your friends, administrators, to upload photos to your Web site; these friends are assigned the administrator role. Other friends are assigned the role of user and can only view the photos.

Finally, security controls work with the membership system to allow valid users to log on, change their password, and to receive a password reminder should they forget a password.

Setting Up Users and Roles

Have you ever developed a Web site and wished to protect sections of your site by requiring visitors to use a password?

Developing a system to manage membership and roles and to provide security controls for all users would literally take hundreds of hours and require thousands of lines of code. Additionally, the data for membership and roles would need to be stored in a secure and robust database such as SQL Server. Fortunately, ASP.NET 2.0 and Visual Basic 2005 provide everything required to utilize membership and roles with minimal effort on your part.

Before using the membership, roles, or security control features in your Web project, there is a little configuration that is required. After creating a Web project in Visual Studio 2005, access the VS 2005 menu, click Website, then click ASP.NET Configuration. This opens the ASP.NET Web Application Administration page for the current application, as shown in Figure 4-17. Selecting the Security tab takes you to the Security form shown in Figure 4-18. The Security form allows you to use the Security Setup Wizard, which walks you through the step-by-step process of creating users and roles. Additionally, the Security Setup Wizard creates the database and tables needed for the operation of the membership and roles system. If Microsoft SQL Server is available, the security database and tables are created in Microsoft SQL Server. Otherwise, Microsoft Access is used. From the ASP.NET WebApplication Administration page, clicking the Manage Users link shown in Figure 4-18 opens the Search for User Web page, as shown in Figure 4-19. The Search for Users page provides the ability to search for users and assign roles to users.

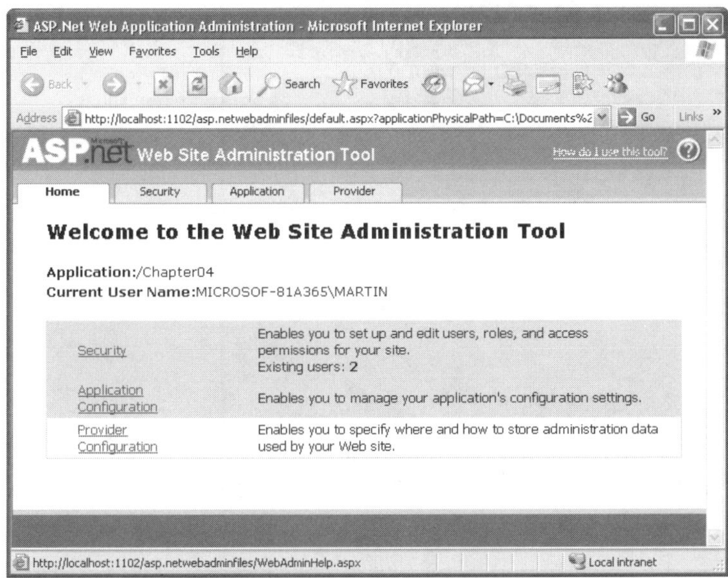

Figure 4-17 Web Site Administration Tool

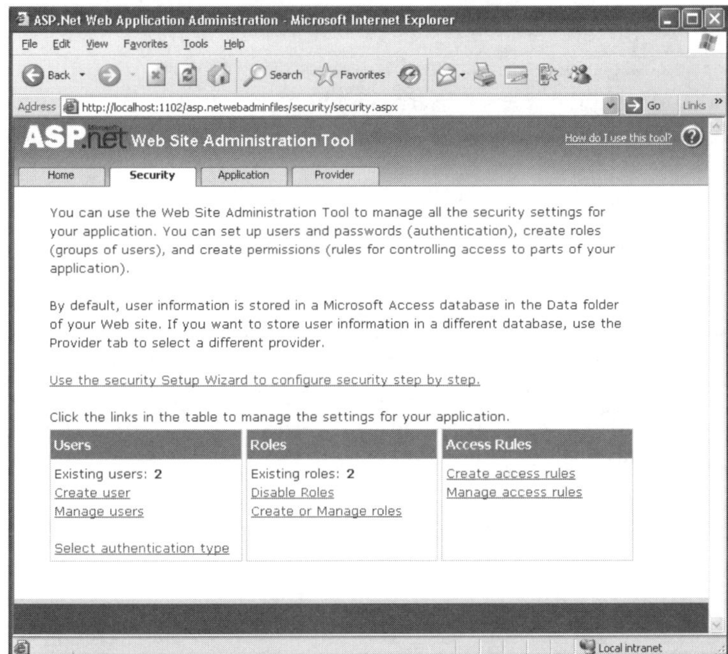

Figure 4-18 Security tab of the Web Site Administration Tool

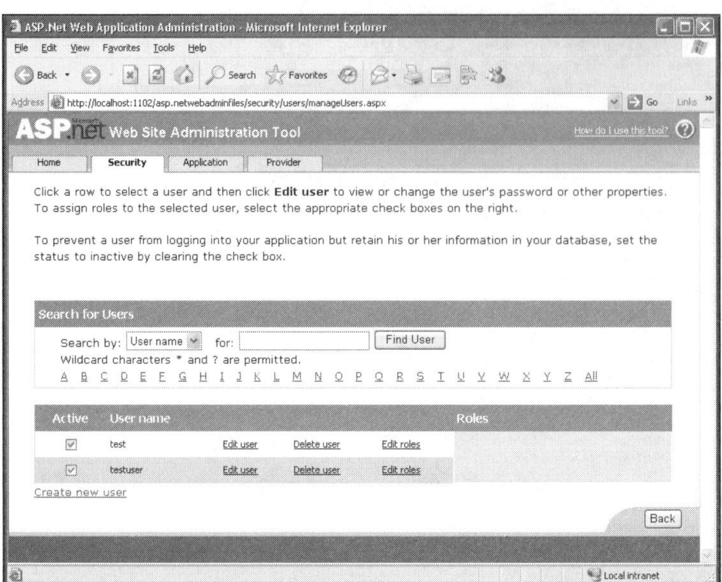

Figure 4-19 Listing users and assigning them roles

Before you attempt to use membership and security controls, you must make sure you have created users for the membership system. If you intend to use roles, you need to ensure that you have created roles and assigned roles to users as is appropriate. Although it is not obvious when creating a user, passwords must be at least seven characters in length and must include a symbol and a number.

Working with Users and Roles in Your Applications

In the previous section, you looked at the basic setup and configuration capabilities provided by the ASP.NET Configuration system so that membership, roles, and security controls can be used. In this section you will begin to use users and roles, as well as security controls in your application. The first item discussed is security controls. The reason for this is that in order to work with users and check for roles, you need the user to log on. The easiest way to do so is with security controls.

Security Controls

There are a number of security controls, and each has a different purpose, as listed in Table 4-1. All of these controls can simply be placed on a page, have their properties set, and be used without any additional code. It just doesn't get much better than that.

Table 4-1 Security controls list

Security control name	Description
Login	The Login control pictured in Figure 4-20 allows the user to specify a username and password and log on. Optionally, it provides the ability to remember the username between sessions. You can optionally show links to a page with the password recovery page and a registration page.
CreateUserWizard	The CreateUserWizard control pictured in Figure 4-21 can be used if you allow users to register themselves on your site.
LoginName	The LoginName control either displays nothing if the user is not logged on (Figure 4-22), or if the user is logged on, this control displays the user login name (Figure 4-23).
LoginView	This control provides two views: one for a user who is not logged on (Figure 4-24) and another for a user who is logged on (Figure 4-25). Each view contains a panel to place the control on. The view automatically displays the appropriate panel based on the user's login status.
PasswordRecovery	The PasswordRecovery control shown in Figure 4-26 makes it easy for the user to recover a lost password. There are several approaches that are supported, such as challenge questions or e-mails with the correct password.
LoginStatus	This control shows whether the user is logged off (Figure 4-27) or logged on (Figure 4-28). A user who is not logged on sees a login link that takes the user to a login page. A logged on user sees a logout link that logs the user off.
ChangePassword	The ChangePassword control pictured in Figure 4-29 allows a user who has logged on to change his or her password.

Figure 4-20 The Login control

Figure 4-21 The CreateUserWizard control

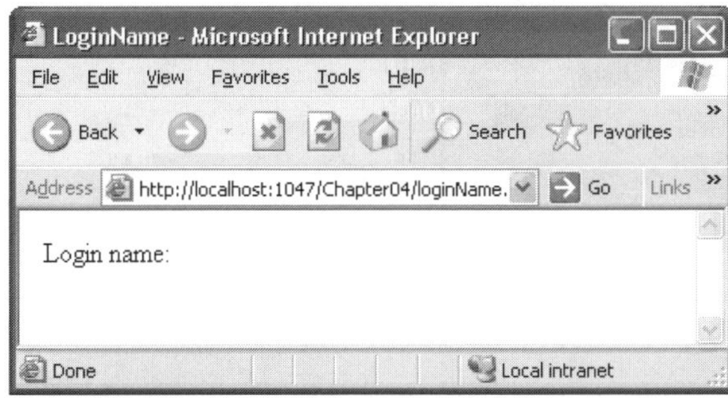

Figure 4-22 The LoginName control with no logged on user

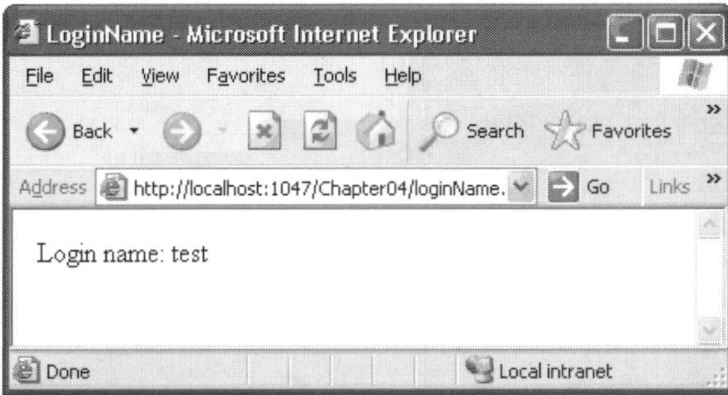

Figure 4-23 The LoginName control with a logged on user

Figure 4-24 The LoginView for a user who is not logged on

Figure 4-25 The LoginView for a logged on user

Figure 4-26 The PasswordRecovery control

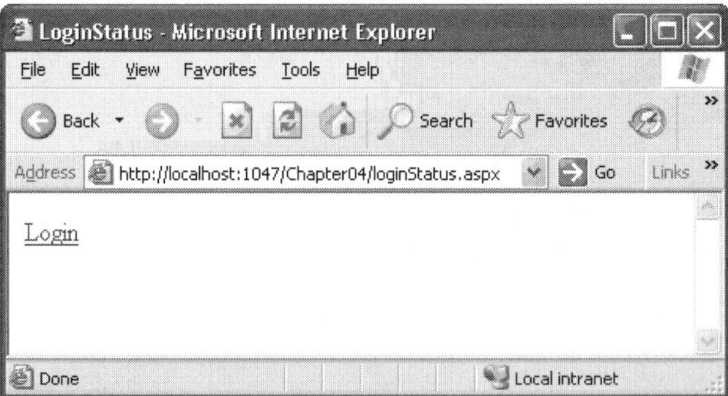

Figure 4-27 The LoginStatus control for a logged off user

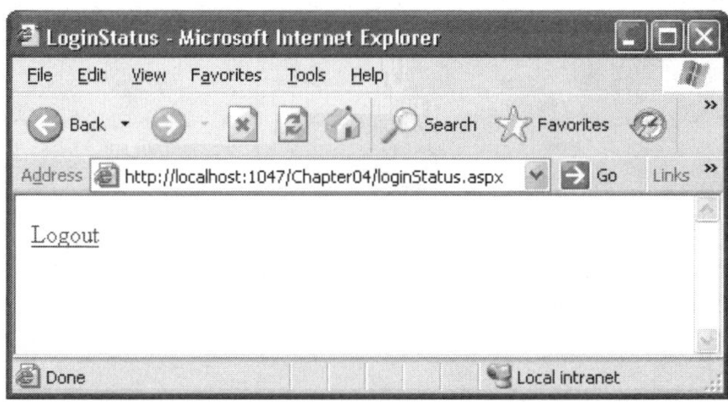

Figure 4-28 The LoginStatus control for a logged on user

Figure 4-29 The ChangePassword control

Many times the term *authenticated* is used to indicate that a user has logged on, and the term *unauthenticated* or *anonymous user* is used to indicate a user has not logged on.

A simple logon and logoff sequence using security controls can be set up in the following manner:

1. Ensure that the ASP.NET Configuration system has been used to create at least one user.
2. To create a new Web form, click **Website**, then click **Add New Item**. Name the page **HomePage.aspx**, and make sure Select Master Page is not checked. Click **Add**.
3. Drag a **LoginView** control from the Toolbox and place it on the form. Click **LoginView** control and type **Would you like to** into the LoginView control. Drag a **LoginStatus** control from the Toolbox and drop it immediately after the text you entered. Figure 4-30 shows what the LoginView control should look like when this step is completed.

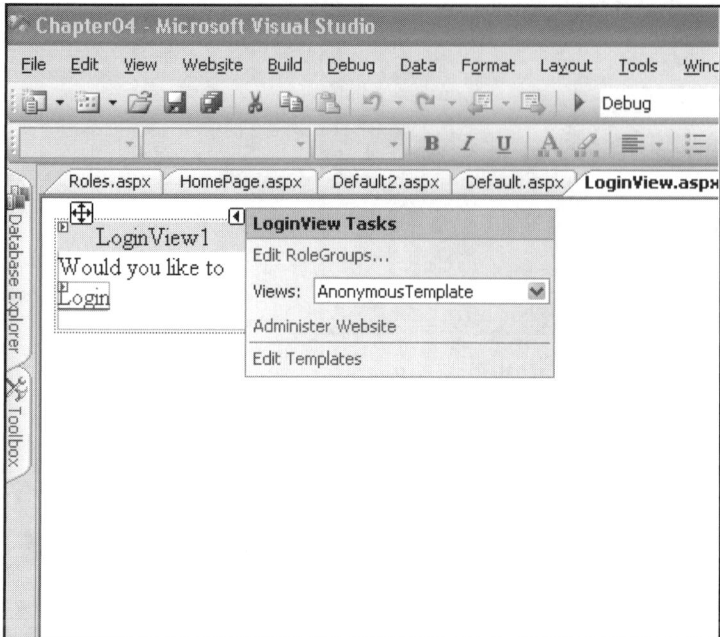

Figure 4-30 The LoginView control for an anonymous user

4. Click the **LoginView** control and click the **small green arrow** in the right corner. In the dialog box that opens, click **Login Template** in the list box. This changes the LoginView control from the view for an anonymous user to the view for an authenticated user.
5. Drop a **LoginName** control into the LoginView control and type **Would you like to** into the LoginView. From the Toolbox drag a **LoginStatus** control and drop it after the text you provided. Figure 4-31 shows what the LoginView control should look like when this step is completed. Ensure that the LoginStatus control displays "Logoff." If the LoginStatus control does not display "Logoff," click the **LoginStatus** control, click the small green arrow in the right corner and select **Logged In**.
6. In the VS menu, click **Website** and then click **Set As Startup Page** to ensure this page opens as the startup page when testing.
7. To create a new login Web form, click **Website**, and then click **Add New Item**. Name the page **Login.aspx**, and make sure Select Master Page is not checked. Click **Add**.
8. From the Toolbox, drag a **Login** control to the form.

If you followed the steps and have configured your site using the ASP.NET configuration system for users and created a user, you should be ready to test. Figure 4-32 shows HomePage.aspx before the user logs on.

Figure 4-31 The LoginView control for an authenticated user

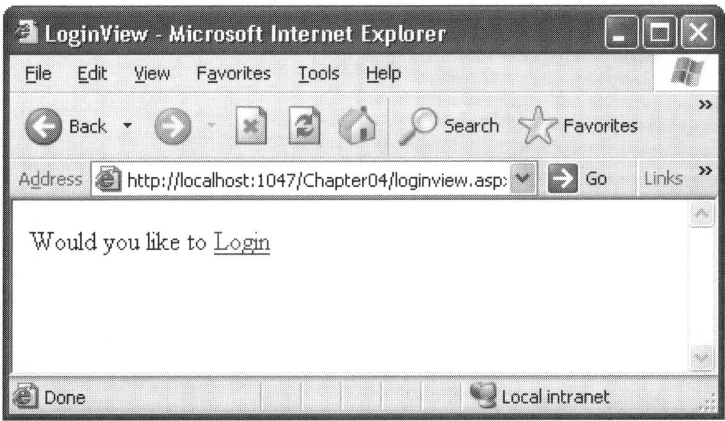

Figure 4-32 No user logged on

When the user clicks the Login link, he or she is taken to the Login.aspx page shown in Figure 4-33. Once the user has successfully logged on, he or she is redirected back to HomePage.aspx, as shown in Figure 4-34. Notice in Figure 4-34 that the LoginView control is now displaying the view for a logged on user. Additionally, notice the LoginName control is displaying the user's login name (in this case *test*), and the LoginStatus has changed to show the logout link.

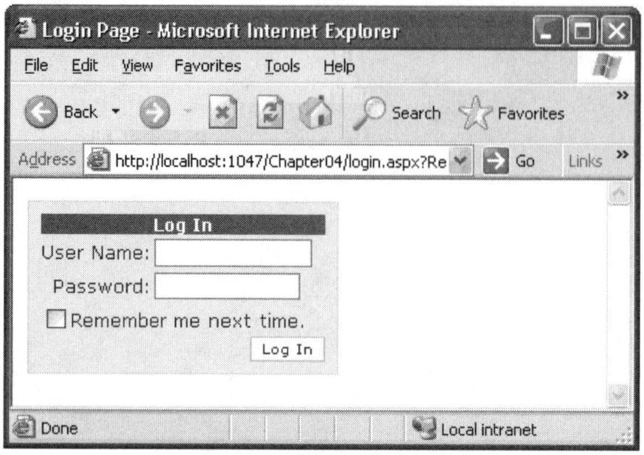

Figure 4-33 Login page

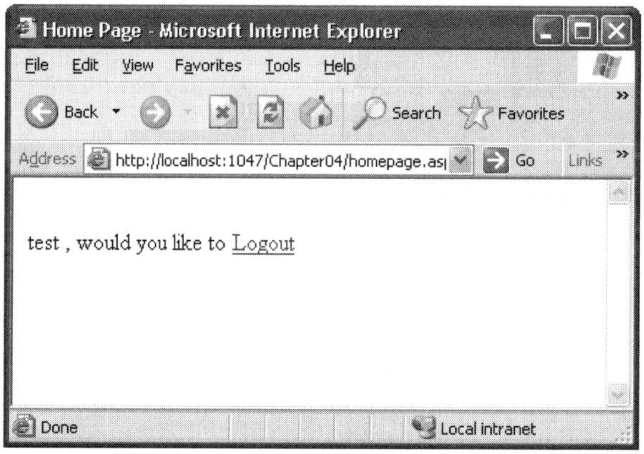

Figure 4-34 User logged on

Instead of using a LoginView control, perhaps you decided to make some controls invisible and then make them visible when the user logs on. By using the My.User.IsAuthenticated property, it is easy to tell if a user is logged on. The following code is from a Web Forms PageLoad event. In this code there are two Label controls that are made visible if the user is logged on and invisible if the user in not logged on.

```
If (My.User.IsAuthenticated) Then
    lblWelcome.Visible = True
    lblMessage.Visible = True
Else
    lblWelcome.Visible = False
    lblMessage.Visible = False
End If
```

Using Roles in Code

Authentication is all about ensuring that only valid users can log on to an application. When a user logs on to an application, he or she is *authenticated*. In many applications there is an additional activity that must be performed. This activity is called *authorization*. Authorization allows a user to perform certain activities or view certain data based on his or her role. The code in the following example is in the Web forms Page_load event. The first line of code makes the upload link button invisible, so that by default no one can access the upload link button. There is then an If statement that grants access to the upload link button by making it visible only if a user's role is admin. Figure 4-35 shows the link is visible for the logged on user because this user's role is admin. Users who have not logged on won't be assigned a role. That is why the Else statement in the code is written—to handle a user who has not logged on.


```
' make sure the default is no access
  lnkBtnUpload.Visible = False

If (My.User.IsInRole("admin")) Then
    lblRole.Text = "admin"
    lnkBtnUpload.Visible = True
ElseIf (My.User.IsInRole("user")) Then
    lblRole.Text = "user"
Else
    lblRole.Text = "not logged on"
End If
```

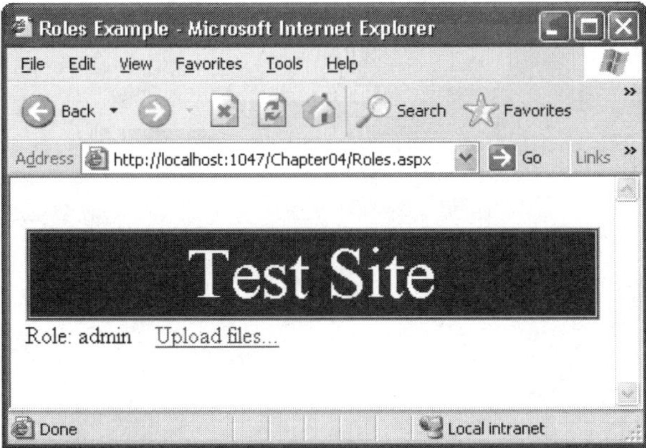

Figure 4-35 Upload is available because the user is an admin

Chapter Summary

This chapter provides details about the new capabilities of ASP.NET 2.0 for building Web applications.

- The new file-based ASP.NET projects make testing and debugging easy and don't require Internet Information Server.
- Master pages allow you to build Web page templates that can be applied to pages within your Web site to give your site a standard look and feel.
- Themes allow for sophisticated management of the fonts, colors, and the overall appearance of controls.
- The new Profile facility allows user information to be permanently stored with a few declarations in the web.config file.
- Membership and security controls allow you to create users, to allow users to log on, and to determine if a user is logged on or not.
- Roles allow you to determine a user's assigned role for purposes of authorization. Once the user's role is known, you can decide whether their role allows them to can carry out certain operations such as uploading a file.

CHAPTER

5

Introduction to Mobile Application Development

In this chapter you will:

- Learn the basics of Smart Device development using Visual Basic 2005
- Recognize the difference between the .NET Framework and the .NET Compact Framework
- Discover the differences between Pocket PC and Smartphones
- Build both a Pocket PC and Smartphone application using Visual Basic 2005 and the provided emulators
- Consider how an application can be designed for both the Pocket PC and the Smartphone

Mobile devices such as personal digital assistants (PDAs) and cell phones are proliferating at an amazing rate. Each day hundreds of thousands of cell phones are purchased. For the most part, PDAs and cell phones have a very rudimentary set of applications that come with them, but each year these devices become more powerful and more capable. Mobile applications are beginning to become more sophisticated: from almost every kind of game to route and trip planning applications that use Global Positioning System (GPS) receivers. There is a keen and growing interest in the development of mobile applications. Mobile applications are unique in that they are designed for devices with very small screens that often have no physical keyboard and only small amounts of memory for applications to use.

Visual Basic .NET 2002 offered the ability to develop mobile applications using the .NET Compact Framework (CF), a version of .NET tailored to mobile devices. Each release of Visual Basic has improved in its support for mobile applications, and Visual Basic 2005 is no exception. Mobile development using Visual Basic 2005 is referred to as Smart Device development.

This chapter serves as an introduction to Smart Device development using Visual Basic 2005 and targeting the Windows Powered Pocket PC and Windows Powered Smartphone. Provided here is a basic overview of Windows Mobile, which is the operating system used by Windows Powered Pocket PC and Smartphone. The role of emulators in developing mobile applications is then addressed. The emulators included with Visual Studio 2005 enable development when you don't have access to an actual Pocket PC or Smartphone.

The chapter then covers the limited system resources that Smart Devices have and how Visual Basic 2005 uses the .NET Compact Framework to work within those limited resources. Because Smart Devices are PDAs and phones, they have small screens and limited memory to run applications. The .NET Compact Framework is designed specifically for Smart Device applications, and this chapter calls out the critical differences between the .NET Framework and the .NET Compact Framework.

The basic capabilities and the differences between Pocket PC and Smartphone development are also explored. Some Smart Device experience will be gained through the development of a mobile version of the minibrowser application for both the Pocket PC and Smartphone. Finally, the chapter wraps up with a brief look at designing an application to have a similar user interface and reusable code while targeting both the Pocket PC and Smartphone.

Visual Basic Mobile Application

Visual Basic 2005 allows you to develop applications for Windows Powered Pocket PCs, Windows Powered Pocket PC phones, Windows Powered Smartphones, or Windows CE devices. With the exception of phone capabilities, developing for the Pocket PC (PPC) and Pocket PC Phone is identical. Using Visual Basic 2005 to develop for the PPC or Smartphone is termed **Smart Device development.** In this text the focus will be on developing for the PPC and Smartphone.

Visual Basic 2005 allows Windows Forms applications to be developed for Smart Devices such as PPCs and Smartphones or Smart Device emulators.

The Pocket PC and Smartphone emulators allow you to test your mobile application even if you don't own a Pocket PC or Smartphone device. In an academic setting, this makes it easy to teach mobile courses with little or no investment in PPC and Smartphone hardware.

Visual Basic 2005 has Windows Mobile as a partner in mobile development. Windows Mobile is the operating system that operates on these devices.

Windows Mobile

Windows Mobile is the version of the Windows operating system running in the Smart Devices or in the emulators. Just as there are versions of Windows desktop operating systems, there are versions of the Windows mobile operating system. Windows Mobile 2003 was followed by Windows Mobile 2003, Second Edition. The version of Windows Mobile that is built into Visual Studio 2005 is Windows Mobile 5.0. As you can see, the naming was changed from using the year the version of Windows Mobile was released to simply using a version number.

Windows Mobile 5.0 provides many new capabilities for developing mobile applications. For example, Windows Mobile 5.0 adds the following capabilities:

- More powerful and graphics-intensive games to be developed using DirectX
- Easy access to GPS receivers for location-based information
- Simple access to digital cameras on devices that incorporate a camera
- Standard dialog boxes for accessing and selecting contacts and pictures

The version of Windows Mobile, or its predecessor Windows CE, that a device or evaluator uses affects what is available to developers using Visual Basic 2005. For example, Windows Mobile 2003, Second Edition, does not provide the standard dialog boxes for contacts and picture selection, so those features can't be used from Visual Basic 2005.

Even if you don't own a Pocket PC or Smartphone or if your Pocket PC or Smartphone has an older version of Windows Mobile you can still develop and test Visual Basic 2005 applications and Windows Mobile 5.0 applications using the powerful emulators in Visual Studio 2005.

Emulators and Devices

An often-asked question is "Do I need a Pocket PC or Smartphone to develop mobile applications?" Visual Studio 2005 provides **emulators** that allow development for the Pocket PC and Smartphone (Figure 5-1). There are also emulators for Window CE. The emulators provide a very rich environment to develop mobile applications. They are called *emulators* because they emulate the actual behavior and operation of an actual device. With each release, emulators continue to improve the emulation of actual devices. Although it certainly is nice to have a Pocket PC or Smartphone device, the emulators allow you to easily develop and test mobile applications.

Windows CE is the version of the Windows operating system for small devices such as PDAs, Smartphones, set top boxes, routers, or just about any small device.

In corporate environments the emulators allow quick development and testing. For commercial and production-grade applications, the final testing should be done on the actual devices.

Figure 5-1 Pocket PC and Smartphone emulators

Comparing the .NET Framework and the .NET Compact Framework

When you are developing applications for Smart Devices in Visual Studio 2005, you are using the .NET Compact Framework. The CF is a scaled-down version of .NET. The full .NET Framework takes more than 19 megabytes of disk space when deployed by a system, which would clearly overwhelm a PPC that has only 32 megabytes of memory. The CF is designed to occupy a mere 1.5 to 3.5 megabytes on the device. This includes a scaled-down version of the Common Language Runtime (CLR) to run .NET CF applications and the libraries that make up the .NET CF (think of the executable code for namespaces such as System.IO and Sytem.Data). Most PPCs and Smartphones sold today include the .NET Compact Framework in read-only memory (ROM) on the device, so no installation or configuration is needed.

When you are using Visual Studio 2005 and its drag-and-drop features, the processes of development for desktop applications and Smart Device applications are roughly equivalent. The list that follows highlights a few of the differences in using the .NET Compact Framework versus the full .NET Framework. Most of these differences exist due to the limited screen size, limited memory, and the lack of a mouse and keyboard on most Smart Devices. In the Compact Framework:

- Some controls are missing, depending on the platform you choose. For example, the TabControl is not available on the Smartphone, and the MaskedTextBox is not available in either the PPC or Smartphone.
- Some components are not available. For example, the FlowLayoutPanel, Table-LayoutPanel, and BackgroundWorker are not available in Smart Device projects.

- Some device-specific controls and capabilities are added. For example, both PPCs and Smartphones support infrared communications. Additionally both PPCs and Smartphones support SQL Mobile 3.0, a version of SQL Server made for these small devices. Additionally, the PPC has an on-screen touch keyboard called the *soft keyboard*.
- Some capabilities, namespaces, classes, and methods of the full .NET Framework are missing. For the most part, this is because of limited capabilities available on most devices. For example, the ability to create Web applications using ASP.NET is missing from the .NET Compact Framework. Why? There are not too many applications that require a **Web server** application to run on a Pocket PC or Smartphone.

2005 Features Support

This book has covered a large number of new features that have been added to Visual Studio 2005 and Visual Basic 2005. Table 5-1 shows these major features and whether or not they are available in Smart Device applications.

Table 5-1 Visual Studio and Visual Basic features available in Smart Device applications

Visual Studio 2005 or Visual Basic 2005 feature	Supported in Smart Device projects or applications
Class Designer	Yes
Object Test Bench	Yes
Application events	No
User and application preferences	No
My	My support is limited to forms, resources, and Web services
Generics	Yes
IsNullOrEmpty	Yes
IsNot	Yes
TryParse	No
Using statement	Yes
Continue statement	Yes
Operator overloading	Yes
MaskedTextBox	No
WebBrowser	Yes
MenuStrip, ToolStrip, ToolStripContainer	No
FlowLayoutPanel, TableLayoutPanel, SplitLayoutPanel	No, with forms being full size most of the time, containers are not provided
Margins and padding	No, without containers, such as FlowLayoutPanel, margins and padding are not needed

Additionally, there are a number of new features specific to Smart Device applications available in Visual Studio 2005 and Windows Mobile 5.0:

- Support for DirectX, which enables the development of high-performance games
- Forms and panels support automatic scrolling, thus allowing their content to be larger than the screen
- Support for accessing and operating cameras on devices
- Additional controls for both the PPC and Smartphone such as the WebBrowser and DateTimePicker, as well as the DataGrid (which is now available on the Smartphone)
- The addition of the SerialPort component to access serials ports
- Access to phone API to initiate phone calls on Pocket PC phones and Smartphones
- Access to the Contact Selection dialog box to allow selection of contacts that have been entered into the device's contact list
- Access to the Picture Selection dialog box to allow the selection of pictures on the device
- The ability to use the Pocket Outlook Object Model (POOM) for Outlook Mobile Access and to use contacts and tasks, as well as creating and sending e-mails

Comparing the Smartphone and Pocket PC

Pocket PCs have a long history and have been available for several years running Windows Mobile and its predecessor (Windows CE). **Smartphones** are much newer. The first Windows Powered Smartphone devices reached the market in 2002. For the most part, Pocket PCs are larger form-factor devices that have more memory, a larger screen, and a more powerful central processing unit (CPU). Table 5-2 compares the resources available on a standard desktop system, a standard Pocket PC, and a standard Smartphone.

Table 5-2 Desktop, Pocket PC, and Smartphone comparison

Resource	Desktop	PPC Second Edition (SE)	Smartphone SE
Input	Mouse keyboard (KB)	Touch screen, stylus, soft KB, sometimes a KB	D-Pad, phone KB, soft keys
Resolution	1024–768 or more	640 x 480 320 x 240	176 x 220 320 x 240
Orientation	Square and rectangle	Portrait, landscape, square	Portrait
Resizable	Yes	Yes	No
Network connect...	Modem or network	Cradle, *Wi-Fi, *Bluetooth *Cellular	Cradle, *Wi-Fi, *Bluetooth, Cellular

Table 5-2 Desktop, Pocket PC, and Smartphone comparison (continued)

Resource	Desktop	PPC Second Edition (SE)	Smartphone SE
Network speed	56 Kbps to T1	20 Kbps to 100 Kbps	20 Kbps to 100 Kbps
Power	AC/battery	AC/battery	AC/battery
Framework	.NET Framework	.NET Compact Framework	.NET Compact Framework
Memory	> 256 MB	Typically < 64 MB	Typically < 32 MB
* indicates optional features			

Pocket PCs typically have a touch screen that supports a stylus that provides capabilities roughly similar to that of a mouse. The Pocket PC is designed for two-handed operation, with one hand holding the device and the other hand operating the stylus. Pocket PCs typically have a soft keyboard, as shown in Figure 5-2. The soft keyboard is a control that appears on the Pocket PC touch screen and allows data entry with the stylus. The Smartphone is designed for one-handed operation. The Smartphone does not have a touch screen and does not support a stylus, but it has a phone keypad. Additionally, Smartphones include a small directional joystick (called a **D-pad**), as shown in Figure 5-3. The D-pad allows up, down, left, and right navigation.

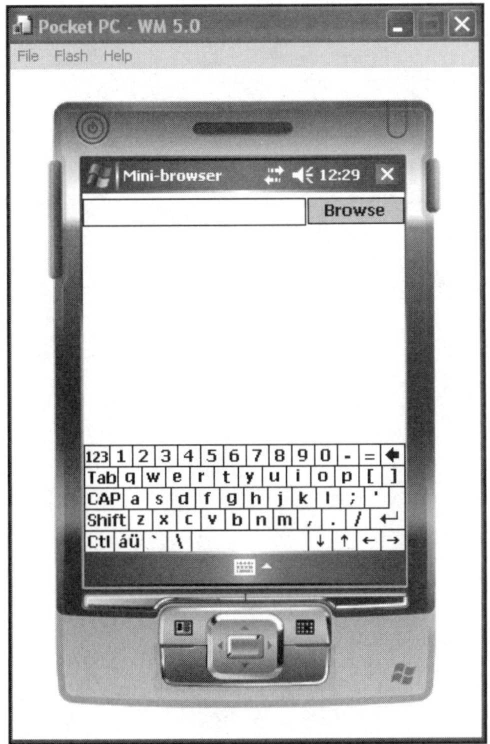

Figure 5-2 Pocket PC soft keyboard

Selecting a Pocket PC or Smartphone for your application depends on the requirements of the application and the needs of the user. Many types of applications are appropriate for both devices. For example, a scientific calculator is useful on both the Pocket PC and Smartphone. An application that allows you to select a state abbreviation and display the state name for that state abbreviation would be useful on both the Pocket PC and Smartphone. On the other hand, an application that requires a fair amount of text to be entered such as a shopping list, journal, or recipes would probably be more appropriate on a Pocket PC. Most Smartphones offer only a phone keypad and don't have an actual keyboard. Many Pocket PCs have built-in keyboards, and those that don't have a soft keyboard for entering data.

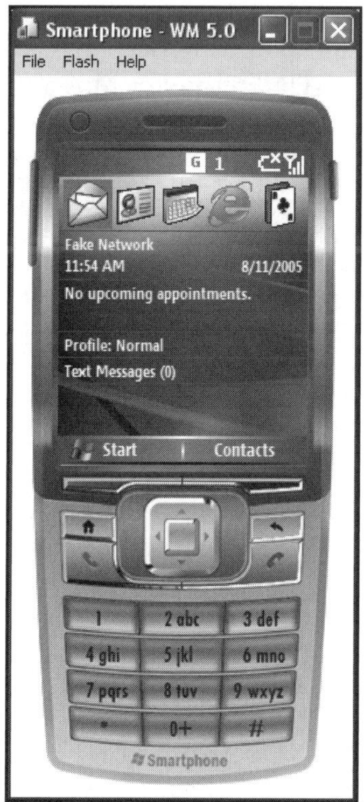

Figure 5-3 Smartphone D-pad

Developing an Application for the Pocket PC

Most of what you know about Visual Studio 2005 and Visual Basic 2005 still applies when developing Smart Device applications. In this section you will build a Pocket PC version of the basic minibrowser application from Chapter 3. It will look like Figure 5-4 when complete.

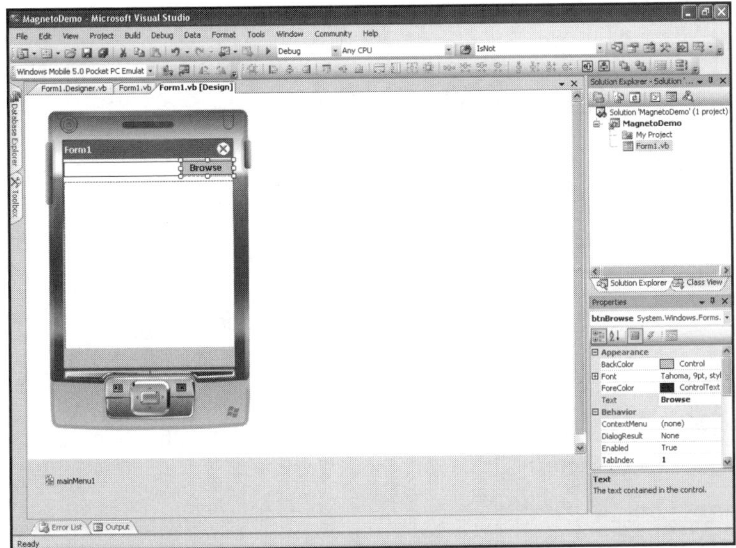

Figure 5-4 Minibrowser on Pocket PC

The steps to build the application are as follows:

1. On the VS 2005 menu, click **File**, click **New**, then click **Project**. The dialog box shown in Figure 5-5 opens.
2. Click the **plus sign (+)** next to Smart Device.
3. Click **Pocket PC Magneto**. This causes a new Pocket PC application to be created. Unlike its desktop counterpart that has a form and a number of classes generated, the mobile application has a single form.
4. Click **View**, then click **Properties Window**. Select the form's AutoScroll property and set it to **True**. This causes the form to have a scrollbar, so the entire area of the WebBrowser can be visible by scrolling.
5. Drag a TextBox control from the Toolbox and name it **txtUrl**.
6. Drag a WebBrowser control from the Toolbox and name it **wbSite**.
7. Stretch the WebBrowser control to be bigger than the display.
8. Drag a Button control from the Toolbox and name it **btnBrowse**.

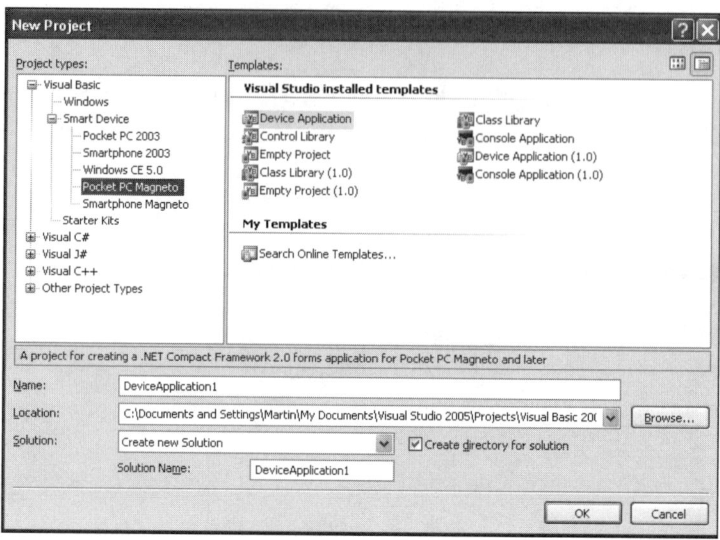

Figure 5-5 New Project dialog box listing Smart Device projects

9. Double-click **btnBrowse** and add the following code:

```
If (not String.IsNullOrEmpty(txtUrl.Text)) Then
   wbSite.Navigate(New Uri(txtUrl.Text))
End If
```

10. Press **F5** to run the application. The dialog box shown in Figure 5-6 opens, which allows the selection of a Pocket PC device or one of the available Pocket PC emulators. Your application should look like the one shown in Figure 5-7.

If you select Windows Mobile 5.0 Pocket PC Device, the application is moved to the device rather than the emulator.

Visual Studio 2005 ensures the emulator or device has the correct version of the .NET Compact Framework to run the application. If the needed files are not present on the device or emulator, they are automatically installed before Visual Studio 2005 starts your application.

There are a couple of differences when developing a Smart Device application as opposed to a desktop version of this application. A quick survey of the Toolbox shows that the Pocket PC application has fewer controls available than its desktop counterpart. In fact, none of the container controls covered in Chapter 3 are available in a Smart Device project. Because Pocket PCs have such small screens and forms are almost always maximized, there is not much need for container controls, so none of the container controls are available. Additionally, the code to navigate to a URL includes the code New Uri (txtUrl.txt). The reason for this is that CF version of the WebBrowser controls Navigate method has fewer overloads, so it doesn't accept strings, but requires a URI instead.

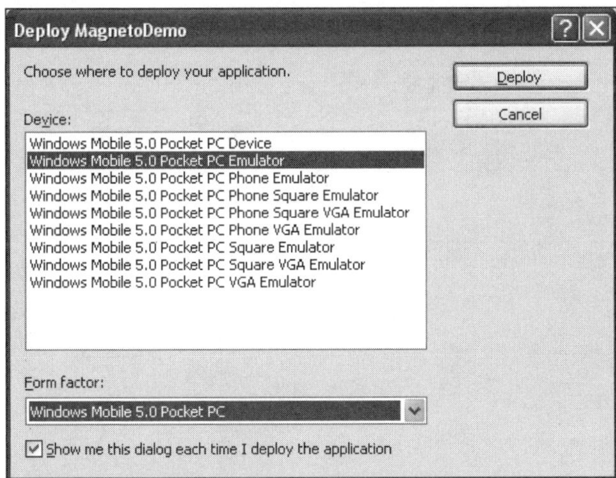

Figure 5-6 Deploy Pocket PC application

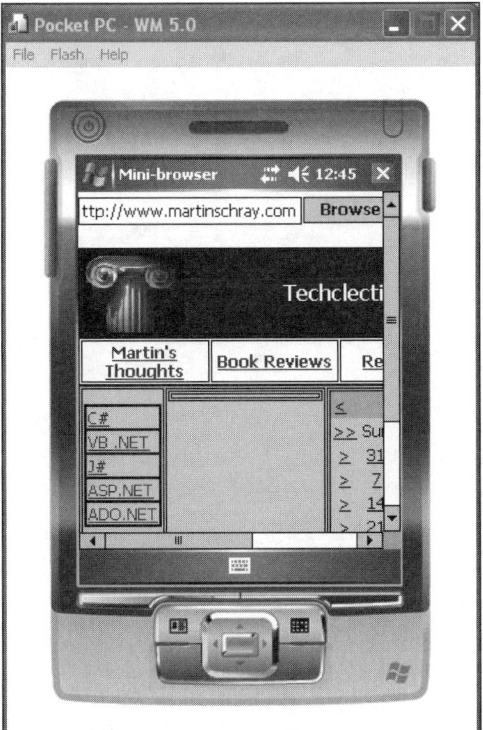

Figure 5-7 Pocket PC Minibrowser application

Developing an Application for a Smartphone

In this section you will learn how to build a Smartphone version of the basic minibrowser application from Chapter 3. It will look like Figure 5-8 when complete. You will notice that building a Smartphone minibrowser application is quite similar to building the Pocket PC version of this application.

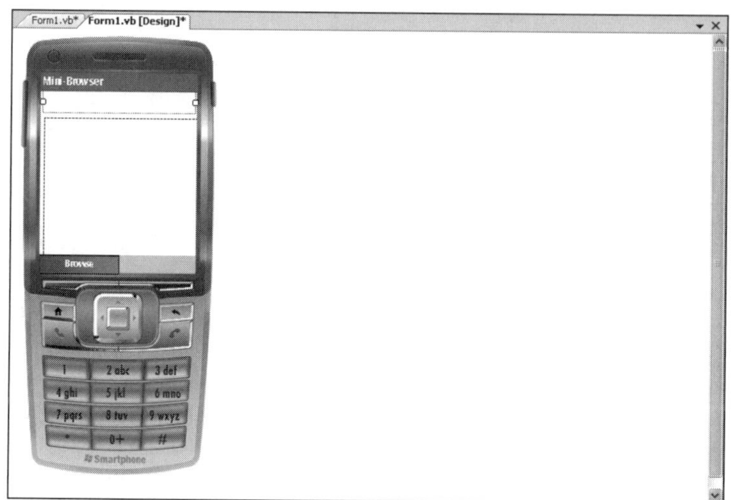

Figure 5-8 Minibrowser Smartphone application

Use the following steps to build the application.

1. On the VS 2005 menu click **File**, click **New**, then click **Project**. The dialog box shown in Figure 5-5 opens.
2. Click the **plus sign (+)** next to Smart Device.
3. Select **Smartphone Magneto**. This causes a new Smartphone application to be created. Unlike its desktop counterpart that has a form and a number of classes generated, the mobile application has a single form.
4. Click **View**, and then click **Properties Window**. Select the form's AutoScroll property and set it to **True**. This causes the form to have a scrollbar, so the entire area of the WebBrowser control is visible by scrolling.
5. Drag a TextBox control from the Toolbox and name it **txtUrl**.
6. Drag a WebBrowser control from the Toolbox and name it **wbSite**.
7. Stretch the WebBrowser control to be bigger than the display.
8. Click the **mainMenu** component and click the green arrow. From the context menu, click **Edit Menu** and add a browse menu item, then name it **mnuBrowse**.

9. Double-click **mnuBrowse** and add the following code:

```
If (not String.IsNullOrEmpty(txtUrl.Text)) Then
   wbSite.Navigate(New Uri(txtUrl.Text))
End If
```

10. Press **F5** to run the application. The dialog box shown in Figure 5-9 opens and allows the selection of a Smartphone device or one of the available emulators. Your application should look like the application in Figure 5-10.

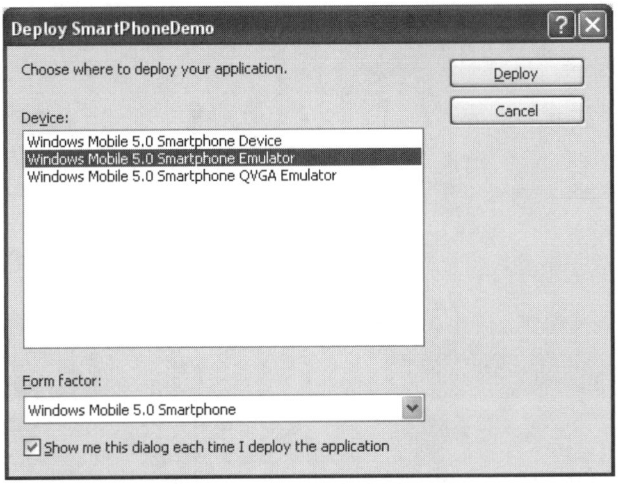

Figure 5-9 Deploy Smartphone application

Like the pocket PC version of this application, there are a couple of differences from what it would be like to develop a desktop version of this application. A quick survey of the Toolbox shows that the Smartphone project has far fewer controls available than its desktop and Pocket PC counterparts. Just like the Pocket PC, the Smartphone has such a small screen that it is almost always maximized so none of the container controls are provided. For the same reasons articulated for the Pocket PC, the Smartphone uses New Uri(txtUrl.txt) rather than a string for the WebBrowser's Navigate method. The Smartphone minibrowser application has a menu item that has replaced the button used in the Pocket PC application. The reason for this is that Smartphones don't have a mouse or stylus, so controls such as ListBox, Button, and TabControl that require a mouse or stylus cannot be used.

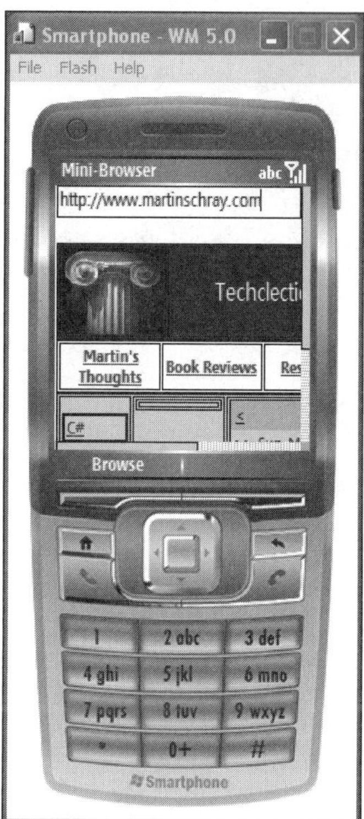

Figure 5-10 Smartphone Minibrowser application

Developing for the Pocket PC and Smartphone

This section briefly explores developing your application for both the Pocket PC and Smartphone. One of the first steps before a single line of code is written is to gather the requirements for the application. The requirements lay out what the application needs to do and what actions and operations the user needs to be able to perform. The requirements should also address what is often called the **user experience**.

User experience relates to whether the application is available as a Web application that offers easy access from a browser, a desktop application that supports offline access and rich editing capabilities, or a mobile application. More and more, the application ends up being a combination of the user experiences, such as a desktop application that also has a version that operates on the Pocket PC or Smartphone.

If the decision is made to develop mobile applications, specific questions should be considered and asked as part of gathering the requirements for a successful application, and again during the design phases before application development.

To better illustrate the value of these questions, the following scenario is provided, using a hypothetical software development company named SchraySoft. The developers at Schray-Soft decided to build an application that will be used on the Pocket PC, Pocket PC phone, and the Smartphone. The developers decided to answer the following questions before writing a single line of code. The application provides a list of state abbreviations. When a state abbreviation is selected, the full name of the state is displayed.

Following is the worksheet that the developers completed:

1. What types of Windows Powered devices will be supported, such as Pocket PC, Pocket PC phone, and Smartphone?

   Answer: This application will be developed for the Pocket PC, Pocket PC Phone, and Smartphone. The main reason for this is that the users of the applications are able to choose if they want to carry a Pocket PC or Smartphone.

2. How will the user interface be similar or different across each device and what controls will be available across all devices?

   Answer: Several designs for the application user interface were considered. The application developers built a chart (Table 5-3) to ensure that the controls they were planning to use were available on the Pocket PC and Smartphone. As the developers reviewed this table, they decided that although the ListBox and Button controls were very natural on the Pocket PC, these controls would not be supported on the Smartphone, as it doesn't have a touch screen or stylus.

Table 5-3 Controls available on Pocket PC and Smartphone

Control	Pocket PC/Pocket PC Phone	Smartphone
ListBox	Yes	No
ComboBox	Yes	Yes
Label	Yes	Yes
Button	Yes	No (would have to use a menu item)
Menu	Yes	Yes

   The developers decided that by using the Label and ComboBox controls the same basic user interface could be used on both the Pocket PC and Smartphone. The developers did note that on the Pocket PC the ComboBox drops down, while on the Pocket PC the ComboBox simply scrolls through the values. Furthermore, the developers realized the ComboBox on the Pocket PC would be operated with the stylus, while the ComboBox on the Smartphone would be operated with the Smartphone directional pad (D-pad).

3. Is there a way that the application can reuse code?

   Answer: The developers decided that the list of states and list of abbreviations could be read in a single file. Furthermore, the developers decided that the code to read the file and load the ComboBox could be the same, because the file format and the type of controls being used in the Pocket PC and Smartphone applications were the same. Additionally, the developers decided that the code to process the state abbreviation selection from the ComboBox control and the code for loading the appropriate state name into the Label control could be reused as well.

To make it easy to use the same code in both the Pocket PC and Smartphone projects, the developers put all the common code into Visual Basic 2005 library projects. They found the details for building a library project in the Visual Basic 2005 online help. This allowed the reusable code to be compiled into an assembly and easily used on both the Pocket PC and Smartphone application.

The completed version of the state abbreviation application for the Smartphone is shown in Figure 5-11, and the application for the Pocket PC is shown in Figure 5-12.

Figure 5-11 The Smartphone state abbreviation application

Figure 5-12 The Pocket PC state application

Chapter Summary

As mobile devices become more powerful and capable, there is increasing demand for mobile applications. There are hundreds of millions of PDAs and cell phones in use each day. This chapter provides details about Smart Device development using Visual Basic 2005.

- Visual Basic 2005 allows Pocket PC, Smartphone, and Windows CE applications to be developed.
- Emulators allow developers to create and test mobile applications without actually using a Pocket PC or Smartphone.
- Pocket PCs are designed for two-handed operations and use a touch screen and stylus.
- Smartphones are designed for one-handed operations and don't have a touch screen or stylus.
- Smart Device applications use a scaled-down version of .NET called the .NET Compact Framework.
- Applications for the Pocket PC and Smartphone can be designed to have a similar user interface and to reuse code.

CHAPTER

6

ENHANCEMENTS TO ADO.NET

In this chapter you will:

- Discover that existing ADO.NET 1.0 code can run without change
- Configure a windows form project to access a database
- Build drag-and-drop forms to access databases
- Construct a form that automatically allows related data in multiple tables to be represented
- Learn how parameterized queries can improve application security and allow a subset of the data in a table to be retrieved
- Consider how using provider factories can allow you to write code to access multiple different databases
- Explore how SQL Server 2005 allows you to run Visual Basic code on Microsoft SQL Server 2005

ADO.NET is a set of namespaces and classes that allow access to databases such as Oracle, SQL Server, and OLE DB-compliant databases such as Microsoft Access. ADO.NET 2.0 has a number of new capabilities, but one of the most important ones is that existing ADO 1.0 code can run unchanged in Visual Basic 2005.

This chapter includes an example of how you can improve your existing ADO.NET code by leveraging the Using statement to make sure the database connection is closed automatically. This chapter covers how Server Explorer has been improved to make it even easier to connect to an existing database. You'll also learn how the new Data Sources window makes drag-and-drop data access a breeze. By selecting tables in the Data Sources window and dragging them onto forms, you can retrieve, navigate, and update database tables with no additional coding. This chapter will also cover how ADO.NET 2.0 makes linking multiple tables together and displaying the relationships between them quite easy.

Although parameterized queries are not new, they are covered to show how you can improve application security simply by using parameterized queries. You will see how to use Visual Basic 2005 to build a parameterized query that retrieves a subset of the rows in a database table.

You will see how provider factories allow you to write code that allows you to easily access data from a Microsoft Access database using the OleDb data provider or Microsoft SQL Server using SqlClient data provider. Finally, you will get a brief introduction to running Visual Basic 2005 code directly on SQL Server 2005. SQL Server 2005 allows stored procedures, user-defined functions, and other database related code such as triggers to be written in Visual Basic 2005.

ADO.NET Quick Review

Before we jump into the ADO.NET 1.0 review let's look at some relational database basics. Databases can be used to store and retrieve application data. Databases can contain one or more tables. Tables are used to store application data in rows and columns. For example, a table that stores student data might have the following columns: student id, student first name, student last name, and student grade point average. The rows in the student table could represent the students that are enrolled in a particular course.

Databases typically contain multiple tables. In the student example just mentioned, there might be another table in the database that stores student contact information, such as address information, phone numbers, and e-mail addresses. There are often relationships between tables. For example, the student id could be used to relate information between the student table and the student contact information tables. The ability to relate data in multiple tables is the basis for the name relation database.

Relational databases support a standard data–oriented language named Structured Query Language (SQL) that allows data in database tables to be retrieved, inserted, updated, and deleted from tables.

ADO.NET is the .NET Frameworks standard library for accessing relational databases such as Microsoft Access, Microsoft SQL Server, and Oracle. ADO.NET allows the full use of SQL statements to interact with relational databases.

ADO.NET 1.0 introduced a major change that centered on support for connected and disconnected access to data. **Connected access** means there is a live connection to the database and every command (SELECT, INSERT, or DELETE) is carried out when the command is executed. Most people are pretty familiar with this approach to data access. The more revolutionary part of ADO.NET is **disconnected data access**. Disconnected data access connects to the database to bring the data local to the PC. The local data is stored in a DataSet object. Changes can be made to the data in the DataSet. A connection to the database can be reestablished, and any changes in the DataSet object can be reconciled with the database.

Although there are more steps in disconnected data access, it is a **scalable** approach that works well when there are many users accessing the database at the same time. Disconnected access is scalable since the connection and demands on the database are minimized, because the database is accessed only to pull the initial data and again to apply any updates.

BACKWARD COMPATIBILITY WITH ADO.NET

One of the major design goals for ADO.NET 2.0 was to improve its capabilities while ensuring existing ASP.NET 1.0 code still worked.

The following code example is written in Visual Studio .NET 2003. It accesses the database in *connected* mode. First the code creates an OleDBConnection to connect to the database. It then creates a OleDBCommand and executes the ExecuteReader to pull all the rows from the Customer table and writes them to the console. Note the use of the Finally statement to make sure the database connection is closed. This same code runs without change in Visual Studio 2005.

6

```
        Dim con As OleDbConnection = Nothing
        Try
            Dim connectionStr As String =
"Provider=Microsoft.Jet.OLEDB.4.0;Data
Source=C:\data\MasterDetailExample.mdb"
            con = New OleDbConnection(connectionStr)
            con.Open()
            Dim cmd As New OleDbCommand("Select * from customer", con)
            Dim dr As OleDbDataReader = cmd.ExecuteReader()
            While (dr.Read)
                Console.Writeline(dr("custname"))
            End While
        Catch ex As Exception
            MessageBox.Show(ex.Message, "Exception")
        Finally
            If (con IsNot Nothing And con.State =_
ConnectionState.Open) Then
                con.Close()
            End If
        End Try
```

The following code example is written in Visual Studio .NET 2003 and accesses the database in *disconnected* mode. It creates an OleDbDataAdapter and uses the adapter's Fill method to load a DataSet with the data from the database. Finally, it uses a For Each Next loop to write the customer name for each customer to the console. This same code runs without change in Visual Studio 2005.

```
        Dim da As OleDbDataAdapter = Nothing
        Try
            da = New OleDbDataAdapter("Select * From Customer",
"Provider=Microsoft.Jet.OLEDB.4.0;Data Source=C:
\data\MasterDetailExample.mdb")
            Dim ds As New Data.DataSet("Customer")
            da.Fill(ds, "Customer")
            For Each dr As DataRow In ds.Tables("Customer").Rows
                Console.Writeline(dr("custname"))
            Next
```

```
        Catch ex As Exception
            MessageBox.Show(ex.Message, "Exception")
        Finally
            If (da IsNot Nothing) Then
                da.Dispose()
            End If
        End Try
```

You can also mix the Visual Studio .NET 2003 approach with some of the new language features, such as the Using statement, as shown below. The Using statement is covered in depth in Chapter 2.) The Using statement ensures that the DataAdapter's Dispose method is called at the end of the Using statement, thereby freeing any resources the DataAdapter was using.

```
        Try
            Dim connectionStr As String = "Provider=Microsoft.
Jet.OLEDB.4.0;Data Source=C:\data\MasterDetailExample.mdb"
            Using da As New OleDbDataAdapter("Select * From 44
Customer", connectionStr)
                Dim ds As New Data.DataSet("Customer")
                da.Fill(ds, "Customer")
                For Each dr As DataRow In ds.Tables("Customer").
Rows
                    MessageBox.Show(dr("custname"))
                Next
            End Using
        Catch ex As Exception
            MessageBox.Show(ex.Message, "Exception")
        End Try
```

These examples have provided the file path to a Microsoft Access database to retrieve data from that database. Visual Studio 2005 provides a Data Sources window that allows database access to be configured in a more reusable manner.

The Microsoft Access database, DatabaseExamples.mdb, can be found in the student downloads section of *www.course.com*.

Configuring Data Access

The examples in the previous section provided the file path to a Microsoft Access database. There are many benefits to using Database Explorer and Data Sources window to configure access to the database or databases your application uses. Using Database Explorer allows you to easily configure access to a number of different databases such as Oracle, Microsoft SQL Server, Microsoft Access, and others. Once you have added a database to Database Explorer you can see its database objects such as tables, views, stored procedures, and functions. The following steps show you how to download a sample database to use in this example, as well as use Database Explorer to set up a connection to a database.

1. On the VS.NET 2005 menu click **File**, click **New**, and then click **Project** to create a Visual Basic Windows application.
2. Using your Web browser, download the Microsoft Access database, DatabaseExamples.mdb, from the student downloads section of *www.course.com*. Place DatabaseExample.mdb into the root directory for the project.
3. On the VS.NET 2005 menu click **View**, then click **Server Explorer** to open it.
4. If necessary, click the **pushpin** in the upper-right corner to pin Server Explorer in place. When Server Explorer is pinned in place, it looks like Figure 6-1.

Figure 6-1 Server Explorer pinned in place

5. In Server Explorer (it might also have the title *Database Explorer*) right-click the item labeled **Data Connections**. On the context menu, click **Add Connection**, as shown in Figure 6-2. In the Choose Data Source dialog box, select **Microsoft Access Database File**, then click **Continue**.

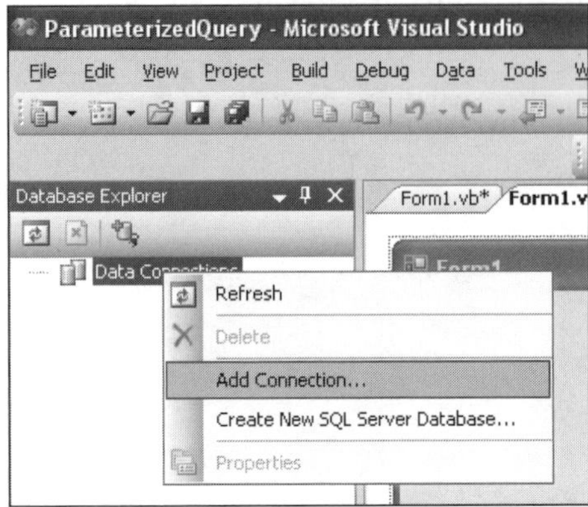

Figure 6-2 Selecting Add Connection from the context menu

6. In the Add Connection dialog box, ensure that the Data Source is set to Microsoft Access Database File (OLE DB). If necessary, click the **Change** button and choose **Microsoft Access Database File (OLE DB)**. Figure 6-3 shows the Add Connection dialog box.

Figure 6-3 Add Connection dialog box with Microsoft Access selected

7. Click the **Browse** button to choose the database file that you downloaded and placed in your project directory. After selecting the database file, click **OK** to create the data connection.

You have now established a connection with the database. This is the first step necessary to access the database in your application. The next process involves using the Data Sources window to add a data source to your application. Follow these steps to add a data source.

1. On the VS.NET 2005 menu, click **Data**, then click **Show Data Sources**. The Data Sources window is displayed, as shown in Figure 6-4.

6

Figure 6-4 The Data Sources window

2. In the Data Sources window, click **Add New Data Source**. The Data Source Configuration Wizard appears, as shown in Figure 6-5.
3. Click the item labeled **Database**, then click the **Next** button. This causes the wizard to move to the next step of selecting a data connection, as shown in Figure 6-6. By default, the data connection you configured in the previous exercise is selected. Click the **Next** button.

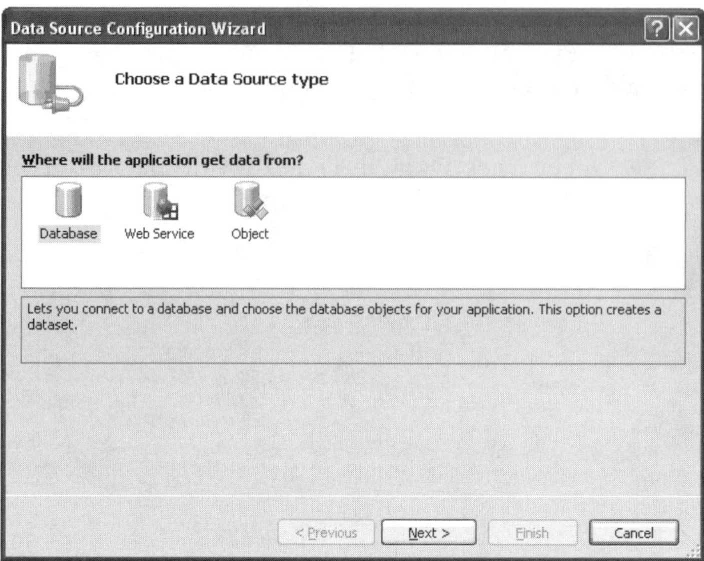

Figure 6-5 The Data Source Configuration Wizard

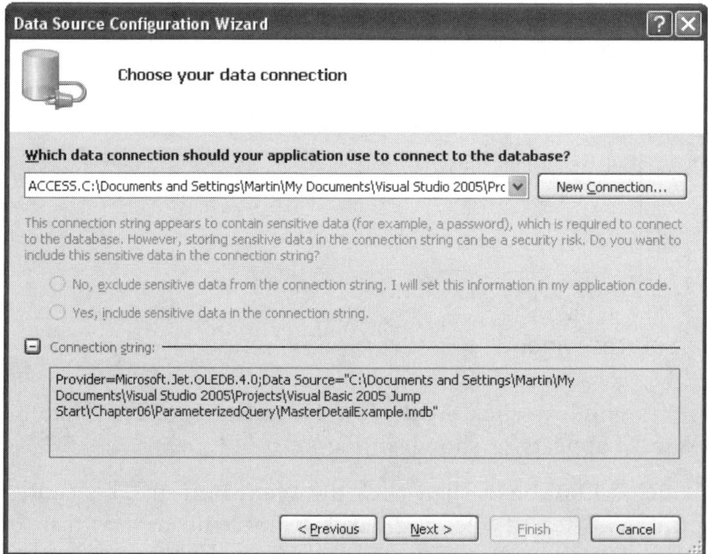

Figure 6-6 Configuring the connection to the data source

4. The Local database dialog box appears, as illustrated in Figure 6-7. Click **Yes**. This causes the database file to be added to the current project.

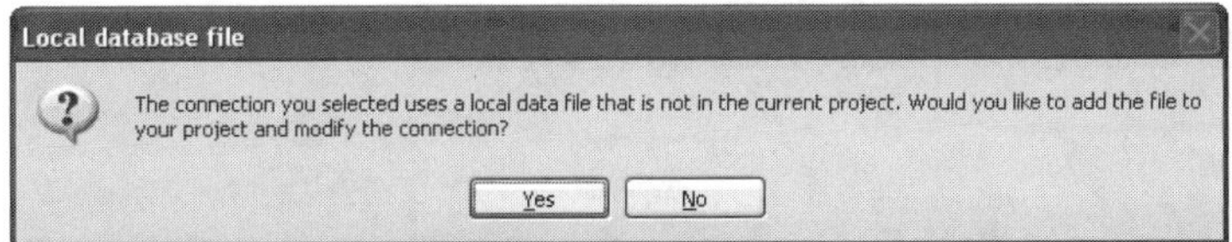

Figure 6-7 The Local database dialog box

5. The wizard now displays a dialog box, as shown in Figure 6-8, that allows the connection string that connects to the database to be stored as an application setting. Make sure the box labeled **Yes, save the connection as** is checked, then click **OK**.

If the save the connection as checkbox is not checked, the connection string won't be stored as an application setting.

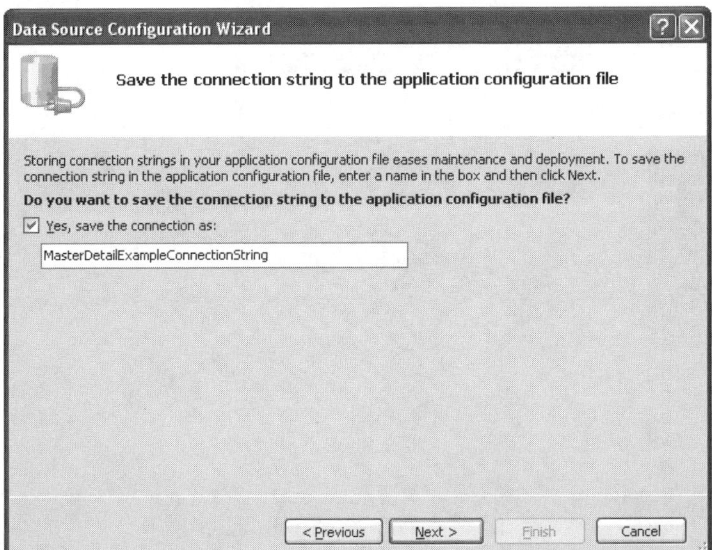

Figure 6-8 Save the connection string to the application configuration file

6. The wizard now shows a dialog box that allows you to select the database objects you want to access. Click the **plus sign** (+) next to Tables, which displays all the tables in the database. Click the check box next to Tables to select all tables, as shown in Figure 6-9, then click **Finish**. Figure 6-10 shows the Data Sources window after these steps are completed. Notice that the Customer and Order tables have been added.

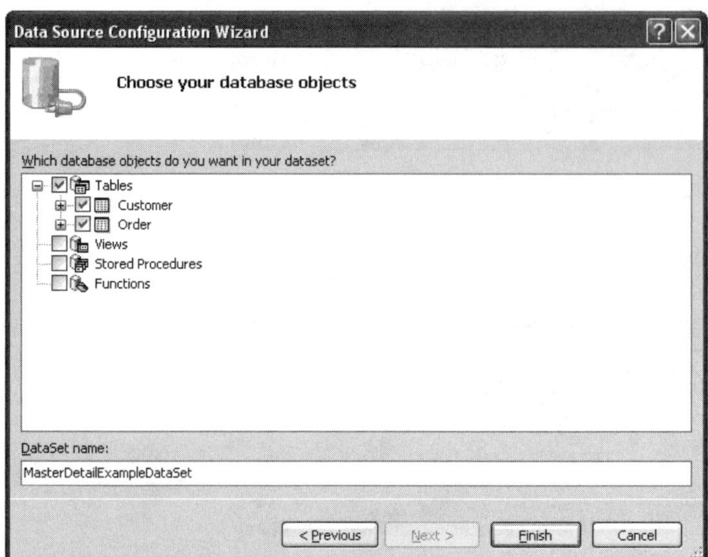

Figure 6-9 Tables in the database

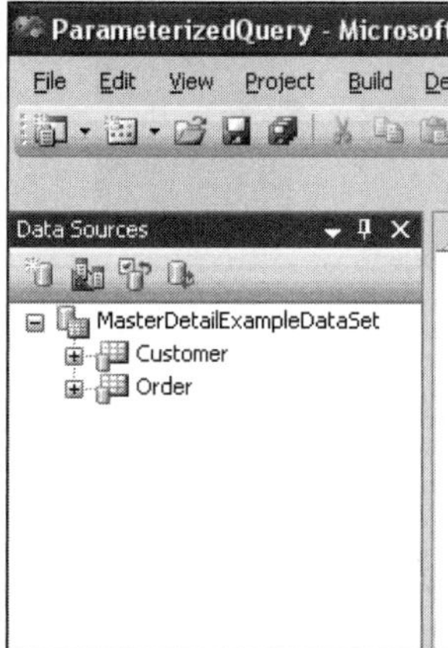

Figure 6-10 Data Sources window now contains the Customer and Order tables

7. If necessary, click **View** on the VS 2005 menu, then click **Solution Explorer**. Use the pushpin to pin Solution Explorer in place. Notice that the database file has been added to the project and a MasterDetailDataSet.xsd file has also been added to the project. The .xsd file contains information about the tables that were selected in the database. Double-clicking the **MasterDetailDataSet.xsd** file opens a designer that allows the tables to be viewed graphically, as shown in Figure 6-11.

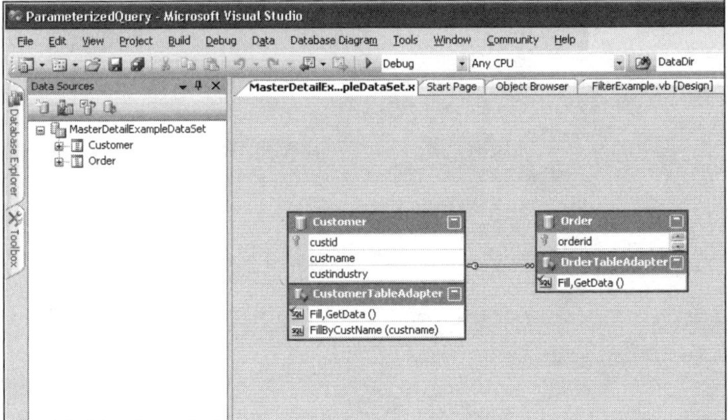

Figure 6-11 Graphical review of the DataTables in the MasterDetailExampleDataSet

8. In Solution Explorer, right-click the project to display the context menu in Figure 6-12. Click **Properties**. This causes the properties for the application to be displayed. Click the **Settings** tab. Notice in Figure 6-13 that a connection string for the database has been added as an application setting.

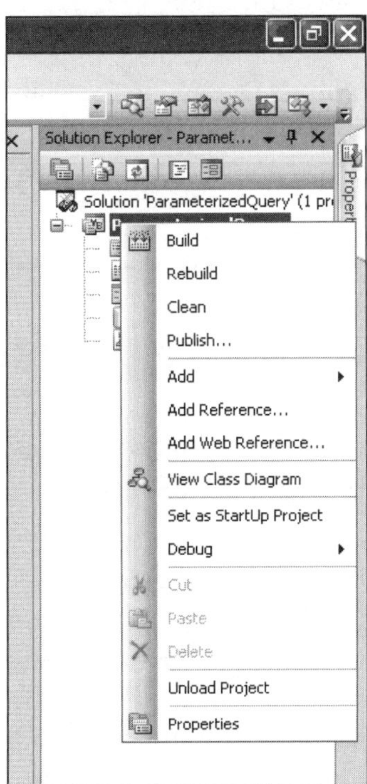

Figure 6-12 The project's context menu

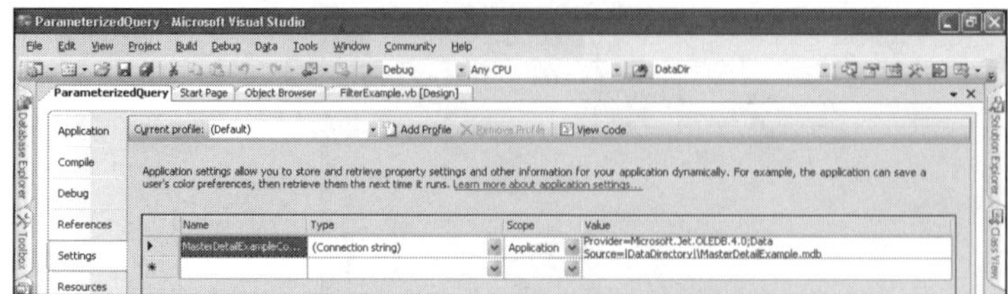

Figure 6-13 The application setting for the database connection string

Once access to the database has been configured, the Data Sources window allows access to databases, Web services, and objects to be configured.

Drag-and-Drop Data Access

Once a connection and a data source have been set up, accessing data is pretty straightforward. The following steps use disconnected data access and assumes that you have performed the steps in the previous section and set up a connection and a data source.

1. On the VS 2005 menu, click **Project**, then click **Add Windows Form**. The Add New Item dialog box is displayed. Name your form **DragDropData.vb**, then click the **Add** button.
2. On the VS 2005 menu, click **Data**, then click **Show Data Sources**. The Data Sources window is displayed.
3. In the Data Sources window, click the icon next to the **Customer** table, then drag it to the form and drop it.
4. On the VS 2005 menu, click **View**, then click **Solution Explorer**. Right-click the project, then click **Properties** on the context menu.
5. The properties for the project are displayed. Ensure that the Startup form is set to **DragDropData**, as illustrated in Figure 6-14.
6. On the VS 2005 menu, click **Debug**, then click **Start Debugging**. The DragDropData form appears, as shown in Figure 6-15.

The application allows data access to the Customer table and has a navigation ToolStrip that allows navigation and interaction with the data in the Customer table.

In Visual Studio .NET 2003, this same basic exercise could have been built. Visual Basic. NET 2003 didn't provide a navigator control and generated three objects to allow data access: OleDbConnection1, OleDbAdapter1, and DataSet11. In Visual Basic 2005, four objects are generated: MasterDetailExampleDataSet, CustomerBindingSource, CustomerTableAdapter, and CustomerBindingNavigator. Figure 6-16 shows the form with the generated objects.

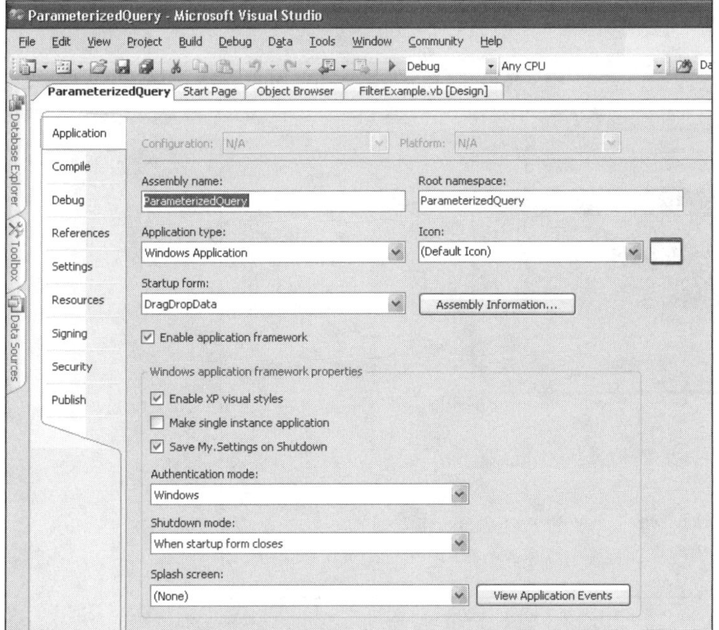

Figure 6-14 Set the Startup form to DragDropData

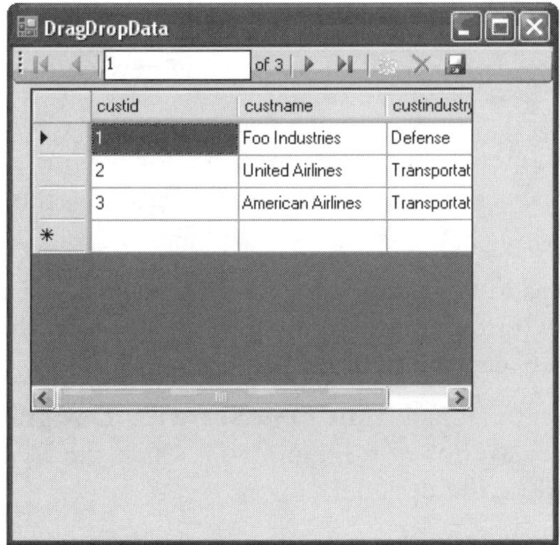

Figure 6-15 The DragDropData application

Master-Detail Made Easy

What if there was a need to see the orders related to a particular customer? Visual Basic 2005 allows these types of relationships between tables in a database to be easily displayed. Displaying this type of related data often is called **master-detail**. In this case, a different

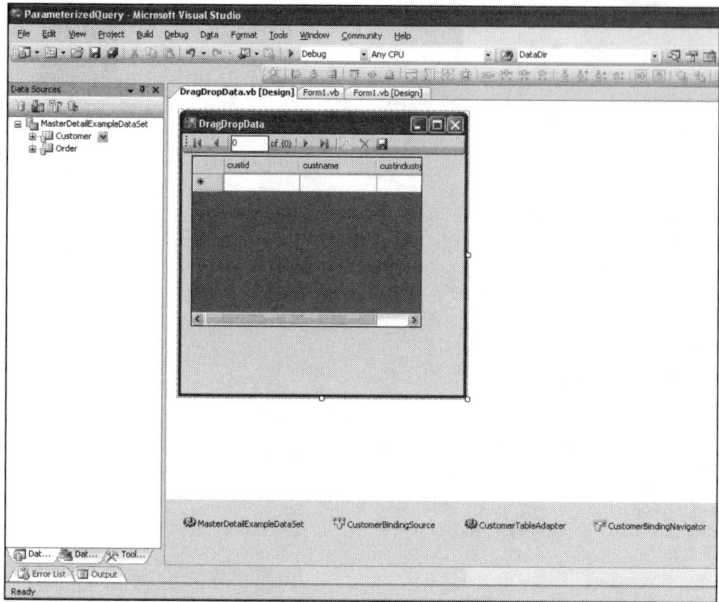

Figure 6-16 DragDropData form with generated objects

master record is selected when the details need to be presented for that master record. For example, for a particular customer (the master record), there are associated orders (detail records). If a different customer is selected, you need to present the new customer-related orders.

The following steps add a master-detail view to the DragDropData form. This allows both the Customer and Order tables to be viewed, and more importantly, it shows the orders for a selected customer.

1. In the Data Sources window, expand the **Customer** table by clicking on the **plus sign** (+). After the columns for Customer are listed, the Order table is listed because there is a relationship between the two tables.
2. Right-click the **Customer** table, then click **Edit DataSet with Designer** to display the tables within the DataSet, as shown in Figure 6-17. Click the **X** in the right corner of the designer to close the designer.
3. Click the **Order** table that is below the columns in the Customer table, then drag it to the form and drop it below the existing Customer table. Figure 6-17 shows the Customer table columns listed, and just below these columns is the Order table that you should drag.
4. On the VS 2005 menu, click **Debug**, then click **Start Debugging**. The DragDropData form appears and looks like Figure 6-18. As you change rows in the Customer table (the master), the rows in the Order table (detail) change to show the orders associated with a particular customer.

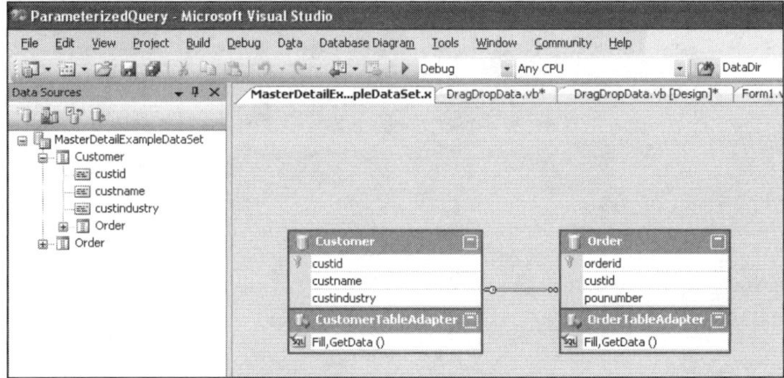

Figure 6-17 Relationship between the Customer and Order tables

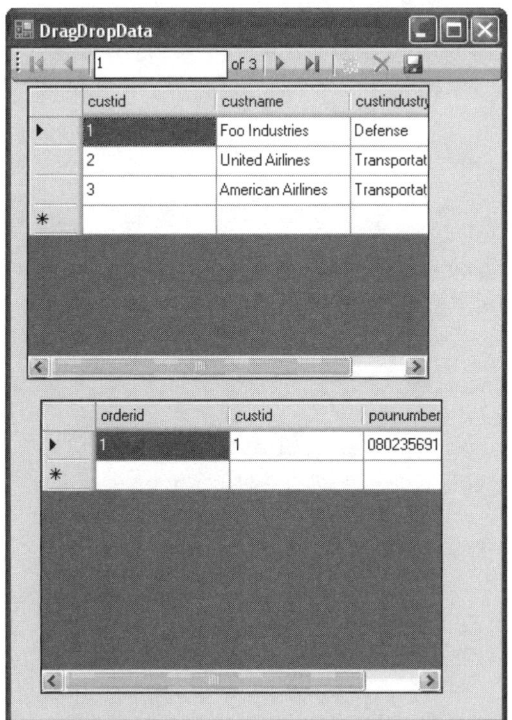

Figure 6-18 DragDropData with master-detail

Using Query Parameters

Parameterized queries are not new in Visual Basic 2005, but they are a greatly underutilized feature in .NET. Say that you want to create a query that returns customers from the database based on the customer name. After some thought you choose to use connected access mode in ADO.NET to accomplish this task.

The simple application in Figure 6-19 was constructed to demonstrate the value of parameterized queries. It consists of a text box, a button, and a list box. The application allows the user to enter a customer name and queries the database to find any matches. Either all matches are listed in the list box or the text "Not found" appears in the list box.

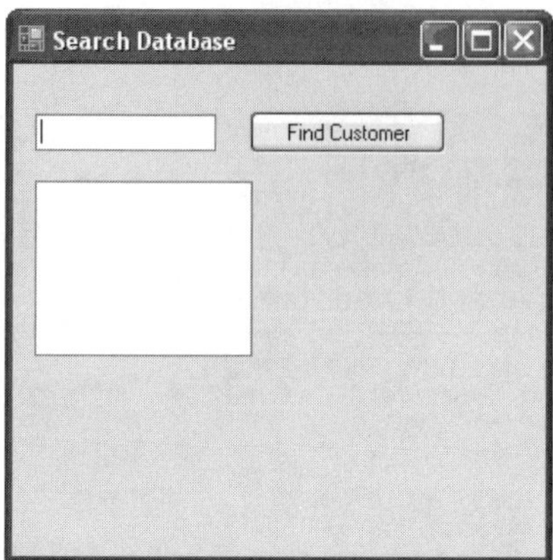

Figure 6-19 Search database application

The following code is executed when the Find Customer button is clicked. Note the use of My.Settings.MasterDetailExampleConnectionString to retrieve the application setting for the database connection string.

```
        Dim con As OleDbConnection = Nothing
        Try
            If (String.IsNullOrEmpty(txtCustName.Text)) Then
                MessageBox.
Show("Please enter a customer name", "Error")
                Return
            End If
            Dim connectionStr As String =       My.Settings._
MasterDetailExampleConnectionString
            con = New OleDbConnection(connectionStr)
            con.Open()
            Dim sqlStr As String
            sqlStr = "Select * from customer where custname = '" & _
                txtCustName.Text & "'"
            Dim cmd As New OleDbCommand(sqlStr, con)
            Dim dr As OleDbDataReader = cmd.ExecuteReader()
            lbResult.Items.Clear()
            If (dr.HasRows) Then
                While (dr.Read())
                    lbResult.Items.Add(dr("custname"))
                End While
            Else
                lbResult.Items.Add("Not found")
```

```
                End If
            Catch ex As Exception
                MessageBox.Show(ex.Message, "Exception")
            Finally
                If (con IsNot Nothing And con._
State = ConnectionState.Open) Then
                    con.Close()
                End If
            End Try
```


This code uses a typical approach, which is to append strings together to build the required SQL query string. In many ways, the code is reasonably well written in that it checks to see if a customer name entered is null or empty and wraps the database access code in a Try, Catch, Finally block to handle any exceptions that occur.

The one major issue with the code is that it simply concatenates the user input with a SQL statement to build a query. Looking at the creation of the SQL string is a bit confusing because of the need to append a single quotation mark after the equal sign and after the value being appended. If there are multiple arguments being used, the resulting string can get pretty complex and even more confusing. The SQL query is constructed in the following code:

```
"Select * from customer where custname = '" & _
               txtCustName.Text & "'"
```

Using parameterized queries this string concatenation can be replaced and simplified as follows:

```
            Dim sqlStr As String
            sqlStr = "Select * from customer where custname = ?"
            Dim cmd As New OleDbCommand(sqlStr, con)
            cmd.Parameters.Add("custname", _
                OleDbType.VarChar).Value = txtCustName.Text
```

Notice that use of the question mark (?) to represent where the parameter is replaced in the SQL statement. The statement `cmd.Parameters.Add("custname", OleDBType.VarChar).Value = txtCustName.Text` sets up the parameter and assigns the value to parameter. When the command is executed, the parameter replacement occurs automatically.

One of the benefits of using parameterized queries is that it is a good first line of defense against SQL injection attacks. The Web site *www.msdn.com* can be searched for *SQL injection* and yields a number of interesting articles on the risks and potential damage that SQL injection attacks can cause and suggests approaches to mitigate these types of attacks.

The basic idea of a SQL injection attack is that an attacker assumes that a field of a form or Web page is used to access a database. By providing malformed input, the attacker attempts to discover or alter information in the database.

In the original code sample, the SQL statement can be manipulated to reveal information about the database or tables in the database. For example, by typing `' or '1=1` into the TextBox control, a SQL injection attack could be mounted. In this case the attacker didn't enter a valid customer name, and in fact, provided a string designed to alter your SQL statements. The application appended the attacker's input to create the following SQL statement `Select * from Customer where custname="'" or 1=1`. Although the customer name was blank, 1=1 is true, so in this example all customer names in the Customer table are returned, as shown in Figure 6-20. Besides a SQL injection attack, if a user enters a customer name that has an apostrophe, such as *Bob's Dry Cleaning*, he or she will inadvertently cause the SQL statement to be invalid.

By using a parameterized query, the additional SQL in the attack is ignored and no results are returned. Additionally, if the user enters *Bob's Dry Cleaning*, the parameterized query makes sure that a valid SQL statement is generated.

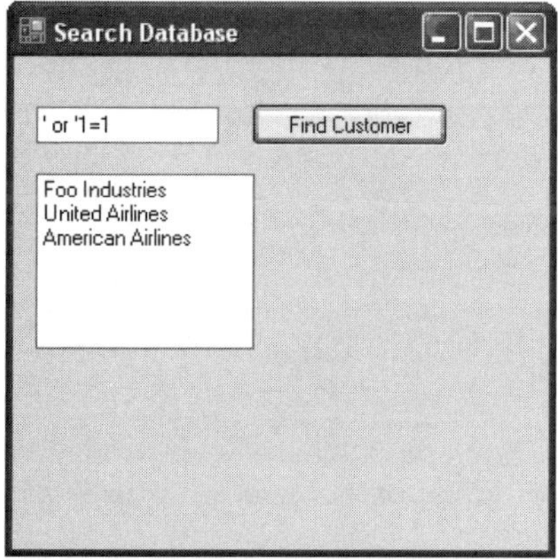

Figure 6-20 Attacker provides malformed input to execute a SQL injection attack

Parameterized Searching

There are often times when a large amount of data resides in the tables of a database. It would take a considerable amount of time, network bandwidth, and database server processing power to return all the rows in a particular table. For example, if the Customer table has 10,000 rows, it would take several seconds or longer to return all 10,000 rows to a client for display. In this situation it would help if a user interface was provided that allowed a customer name to be entered and a subset of the data to be returned.

Visual Basic 2005 can build ToolStrips that use parameterized queries to retrieve subsets of data stored in database tables. The following example shows you how to build a parameterized query that allows you to return a subset of the data found in the Customer table.

1. Ensure the project created earlier in this chapter is opened.
2. On the VS 2005 menu click **Project**, then click **Add Windows Form**. The Add New Item dialog box is displayed. Name your form **FilterExample.vb**, then click the **Add** button.
3. On the VS 2005 menu, click **Data**, then click **Show Data Sources**.
4. In the Data Sources window, click on the **icon** next to the Customer table, then drag it to the form and drop it.
5. Right-click the **CustomerTableAdapter**, which is located in the tray beneath the form, then click **Add Query**. The Search Criteria Builder is displayed, as shown in Figure 6-21. Type **FillByCustName** into the New query name TextBox control.

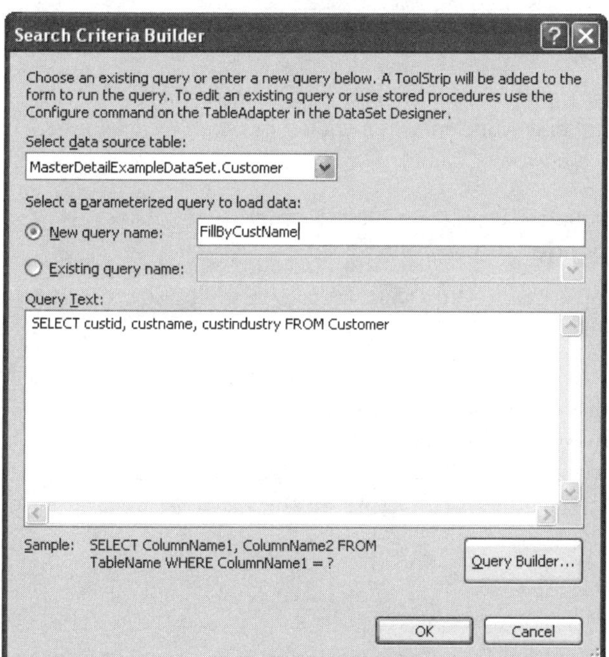

Figure 6-21 Search Criteria Builder

6. Replace SQL statement **SELECT custid, custname, custindustry FROM Customer** in the Query Text (Figure 6-21) with the following SQL statement:

```
SELECT custid, custname, custindustry FROM Customer WHERE
custname LIKE ?
```

7. Click **OK**. A new ToolStrip named FillByCustNameToolStrip is added to the form. The ToolStrip will have a button with the text FillByCustName.

The SQL Like predicate allows the comparison of two strings for partial matches. To do partial matching of a character string in OleDB, use the percent symbol (%). To use partial matching for SqlClient, the asterisk (*) is used. For example, in OleDb if a user entered *Alex%*, any customer name that started with Alex (e.g., Alexander Inc., AlexStore, and AlexWorld) would be returned.

8. Double-click the **FillByCustName ToolStripButton**, then modify the generated code by adding **& "%"** as shown in bold face here:

```
Try
    Me.CustomerTableAdapter.FillByCustName( _
        Me.MasterDetailExampleDataSet.Customer, _
         CustnameToolStripTextBox.Text & "%")
Catch ex As System.Exception
    System.Windows.Forms.MessageBox.Show(ex.Message)
End Try
```

Appending the percent sign (%) to the end of the string pulled from the ToolStripTextBox control also works in conjunction wfith the SQL Like predicate to partially match a customer name.

9. On the VS 2005 menu, click **View**, then click **Solution Explorer**. Right-click the project, then click **Properties** in the context menu.
10. The properties for the project are displayed. Ensure that the Startup form is set to **FilterExample**.
11. On the VS 2005 menu click **Debug**, then click **Start Debugging**. The FilterExample form appears and looks like Figure 6-22. Type **Foo** in the text box next to custname, then click **FillByCustName**. The data is searched, and one matching row is returned, as shown in Figure 6-23. Delete the value in the text box, then click the **FillByCustName** button to restore all the data.

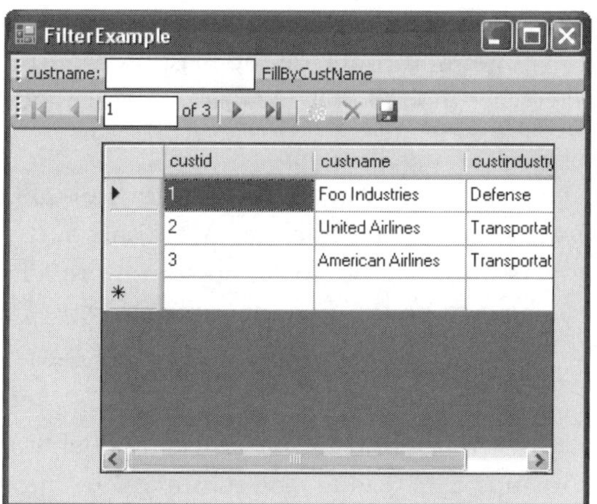

Figure 6-22 The FilterExample form can be searched using the FillByCustName button

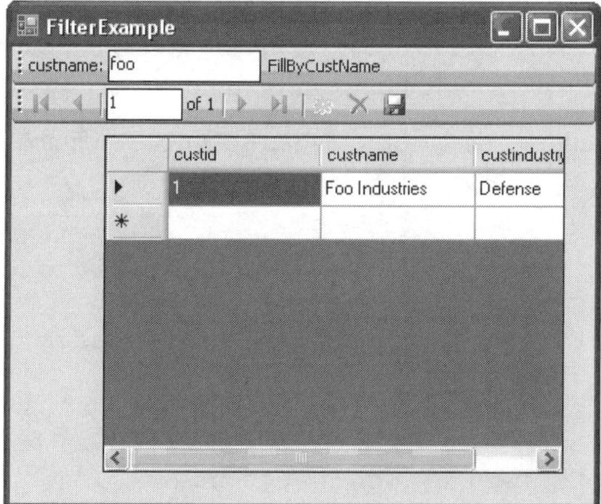

Figure 6-23 The customer named Foo was located

Provider Factories

Provider factories make it very easy to switch database providers. **Database providers** are the classes and interfaces that provide access to a data source. For example, OleDb is the provider that provides access to OleDb-compliant data sources such as Microsoft Access Databases. SqlClient is the provider that provides access to Microsoft SQL Server.

It is not uncommon to change database providers during the lifetime of an application. For example, perhaps an application was originally written using the OleDB provider to access a Microsoft Access database. As the application grows, the requirements for the database grow as well. The developers find they need the power of a server database and choose Microsoft SQL Server. This usually means going through all the existing database code and changing it to use SqlClient namespace rather than OleDb database provider and the classes in OleDb namespace.

Additionally, it is not uncommon that an application needs to support multiple providers. For example, a customer can choose whether to use Oracle or Microsoft SQL Server for their database. This means that developers must be able to support both providers in their application. In ADO.NET 1.0 and 1.1 this was pretty difficult and usually meant building highly customized classes to handle the different classes needed to use the OracleClient and SqlClient.

A **factory** is a specialized class that returns the right database provider (OleDB, SqlClient) and types of objects (connections, commands, data readers, and so on) for that provider. The best way to understand the functionality of provider factories is to look at an example in three parts. The first part of the example accesses a Microsoft Access database using the OleDb database provider. The second part of the example accesses a Microsoft SQL Server database using the SqlClient database provider. Finally, the database access code is rewritten to use a provider factory, so either OleDb or SqlClient can be used to access the data.

The following code uses OleDb to retrieve data from a Microsoft Access database:

```
        Dim con As OleDbConnection = Nothing
        Try
            Dim connectionStr As String = "Provider=Microsoft.
Jet.OLEDB.4.0;Data Source='C:
\Documents and Settings\Martin\My Documents\Visual Studio 2005\
Projects\Visual Basic 2005 Jump Start\Chapter06\
BasicDatabaseExample\BasicDatabaseExample\db.mdb';
Persist Security Info=True"
            con = New OleDbConnection(connectionStr)
            con.Open()
            Dim cmd As New OleDbCommand( _
"Select * from Students", con)
            Dim dr As OleDbDataReader = cmd.ExecuteReader()
            While (dr.Read)
                Console.WriteLine(dr("name"))
            End While
        Catch ex As Exception
            MessageBox.Show(ex.Message, "Exception")
        Finally
            If (con IsNot Nothing And con.State = _
                    ConnectionState.Open) Then
                con.Close()
            End If
        End Try
```

The next code has been rewritten to access the same table now residing in Microsoft SQL Server. Notice that OleDbConnection, OleDbCommand, and OleDbDataReader have been replaced by the SqlClient classes SqlConnection, SqlCommand, and SqlDataReader. The other change is the use of a connection string for SQL Server:

```
        Dim con As SqlConnection = Nothing
        Try
            Dim connectionStr As String = "Data Source=.
\SQLEXPRESS;AttachDbFilename='C:
\Documents and Settings\Martin\My Documents\Visual Studio 2005\
Projects\Visual Basic 2005 Jump Start\Chapter06\
MasterDetailExample\MasterDetailExample\test.mdf';
Integrated Security=True;User Instance=True"
            con = New SqlConnection(connectionStr)
            con.Open()
            Dim cmd As New SqlCommand( _
"Select * from Students", con)
            Dim dr As SqlDataReader = cmd.ExecuteReader()
            While (dr.Read)
                Console.WriteLine(dr("name"))
            End While
        Catch ex As Exception
            MessageBox.Show(ex.Message, "Exception")
        Finally
            If (con IsNot Nothing And con.State = _
ConnectionState.Open) Then
                con.Close()
            End If
        End Try
```


Using provider factories, the code in the OleDb and SqlClient examples can be combined and written to support the use of either provider. The following code uses the provider factory to get the correct provider, then uses the returned provider factory to create the objects (connections, commands, and data readers) to access that provider. The GenericDataAccess method takes two arguments. The first is the name of the provider, and the second is the connection string for the database. The name of the provider is passed to the DbProviderFactories.GetFactory shared method to get the factory for the requested provider. Then the factory is used to create the required connection, command, and data reader. For example, dbFactory.CreateConnection returns a connection object appropriate for the selected provider:

```
    Public Sub GenericDataAccess(ByVal provider As String, ByVal
connectionStr As String)
        Dim dbFactory As DbProviderFactory = _
DbProviderFactories.GetFactory(provider)
        Dim con As IDbConnection = Nothing
        Try
            con = dbFactory.CreateConnection
            con.ConnectionString = connectionStr
            con.Open()
```

```
                Dim cmd As IDbCommand
                cmd = dbFactory.CreateCommand
                cmd.CommandText = "Select * from Students"
                cmd.Connection = con
                Dim dr As IDataReader = cmd.ExecuteReader()
                While (dr.Read)
                    Console.WriteLine(dr("name"))
                End While
            Catch ex As Exception
                MessageBox.Show(ex.Message, "Exception")
            Finally
                If (con IsNot Nothing And con.State = _
ConnectionState.Open) Then
                    con.Close()
                End If
            End Try
```

If the developer needs to use the OleDb provider to access a Microsoft Access database, he or she can call GenericDataAccess as follows:

```
GenericDataAccess("System.Data.OleDb,_
"Provider=Microsoft.Jet.OLEDB.4.0;Data Source='C:
\Documents and Settings\Martin\My Documents\Visual Studio 2005\
Projects\Visual Basic 2005 Jump Start\Chapter06\
BasicDatabaseExample\BasicDatabaseExample\db.mdb';
Persist Security Info=True")
```

If the SqlClient provider was required, the developer could call GenericDataAccess as follows:

```
GenericDataAccess("System.Data.SqlClient",_
"Data Source=.\SQLEXPRESS;AttachDbFilename='C:
\Documents and Settings\Martin\My Documents\Visual Studio 2005\
Projects\Visual Basic 2005 Jump Start\Chapter06\
MasterDetailExample\MasterDetailExample\test.mdf';
Integrated Security=True;User Instance=True")
```

Visual Basic 2005 in a Database Near You

Most Visual Basic developers have some experience in interacting with databases. ADO. NET makes accessing relational databases relatively straightforward. Most relational databases also have their own programming languages. For example, Microsoft SQL Server has Transact-SQL (referred to as T-SQL). It is often more efficient to use the programming language of the database than to access data using ADO.NET from your Windows forms application. For example, stored procedures can be written in the database's programming language. They are compiled and highly optimized by the database to execute quickly. The database builds a query plan, which allows the database to know the best approach in which to quickly execute the stored procedure and access the database tables the stored procedure refers to.

SQL statements that don't use database-stored procedures or database user-defined functions are termed "dynamic SQL" statements. Each time dynamic SQL statements are received, the database has to receive the SQL statement, make sense of it, validate it, quickly build a query plan, and then execute the SQL statement.

For dynamic SQL statements coming from a client application, a rough query plan must be built by the server each time a query is sent to the server from the client. For example, if ADO.NET was used to submit the dynamic SQL statement "SELECT * from Student" to the database, the database has to receive the SQL statement, make sense of it, validate it, quickly build a query plan, and then execute the SQL statement using the query plan. If the same dynamic SQL statement was sent to the database again, it would have to go through all these steps again.

In some situations that involve complex SQL statements, a stored procedure might be up to 10 times faster than submitting dynamic SQL statements from the client application. The following is an example of a T-SQL-stored procedure designed to retrieve all the student names from a student table:

```
CREATE PROCEDURE GetStudents
as
SELECT name from student
```

Databases also allow user-defined functions to be written inside a database using the database's programming language. An example of a T-SQL user-defined function is shown here:

```
CREATE FUNCTION TSQLCount   (    )
RETURNS INTEGER
AS
   BEGIN
  RETURN (Select COUNT(*) FROM STUDENT)
   END
```

The issue is that many developers are reluctant to learn yet another programming language. What most developers want to do is to be able to write Visual Basic code directly in the database. It seems the ideal situation would be to use Visual Basic in your Windows form application and use it as the database programming language.

Microsoft SQL Server 2005 has a feature called the SQLCLR, which stands for the Structured Query Language Common language Runtime. The SQLCLR allows C# and Visual Basic code to run on the database server. Talk about cutting down the learning curve for programming the database. If you are using Visual Studio Team Suite and have SQL Server 2005 installed, when you open the new project dialog, you will notice there is an option for database project types (Figure 6-24).

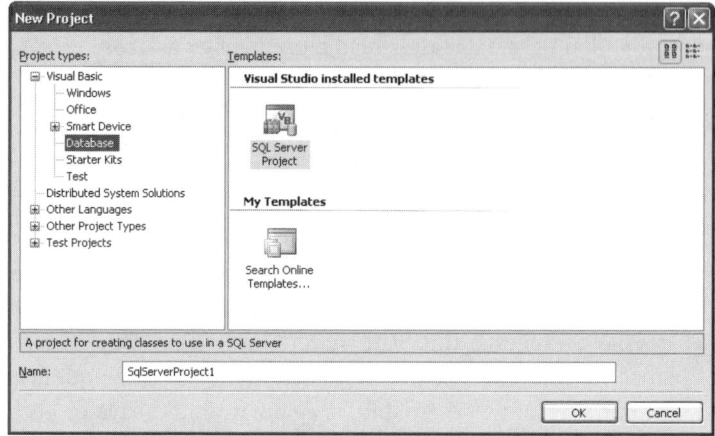

Figure 6-24 Creating a new Database project

Once a database project is made, creating user-defined functions, stored procedures, aggregate functions, triggers, and user-defined types written in Visual Basic are pretty straightforward. The VS 2005 Project menu offers menu items to create each of these types of database objects (Figure 6-25).

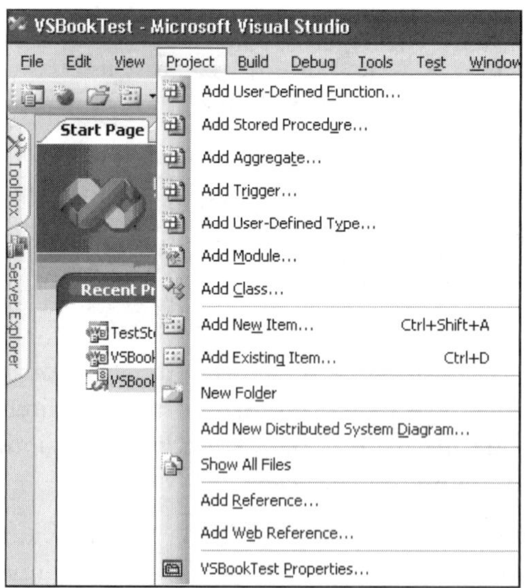

Figure 6-25 Choices for adding Visual Basic code to a SQL Server 2005 database

When you run the database project (by pressing F5), the Visual Basic code for the stored procedure, user-defined function, and other database objects written in Visual Basic are compiled and automatically deployed to your SQL Server 2005 database. Once they are deployed on SQL Server 2005, you can access them in your Visual Basic Windows form, Web forms or Smart Device (mobile) applications.

The T-SQL stored–procedure and the T-SQL user-defined function listed earlier in this section could be written as a Visual Basic–stored procedure and a Visual Basic user-defined function. This is shown in the following example. The SqlConnection object uses a connection string of "context connection=true". Using the context connection means you are reusing the connection that the caller used to invoke the stored procedure or user-defined function in the database.


```
Partial Public Class StoredProcedures
    <Microsoft.SqlServer.Server.SqlProcedure()> _
    Public Shared Sub  GetStudents()
        Using conn As New SqlConnection( _
"context connection=true")
            conn.Open()
            Dim cmd As New SqlCommand( _
"SELECT name FROM student", conn)
            SqlContext.Pipe.ExecuteAndSend(cmd)
        End Using
    End Sub
End Class
Partial Public Class UserDefinedFunctions
    <Microsoft.SqlServer.Server.SqlFunction( _
DataAccess:=DataAccessKind.Read)> _
    Public Shared Function SQLCLRStudentCount() As Integer
        Using conn As New SqlConnection( _
"context connection=true")
            conn.Open()
            Dim cmd As New SqlCommand( _
"SELECT COUNT(*) FROM student", conn)
            Return Convert.ToInt32(cmd.ExecuteScalar())
        End Using
    End Function
End Class
```

The code used to access your stored procedure or user-defined function is very similar to what you would normally write, using SqlConnection and SqlCommand. The difference is that instead of providing a SQL statement to pass to the server, you provide a SQL statement to invoke a stored procedure or user-defined function, which resides on the server. The code to access the stored procedure and user-defined function from your Visual Basic Windows form application would look like the following:

```
            conn = New SqlConnection("Data Source=MSSERVER;
Initial Catalog=test;Integrated Security=True;Pooling=False")
            conn.Open()
            cmd = New SqlCommand("GetStudents", conn)
            rdr = cmd.ExecuteReader
```

```
            Do While (rdr.Read())
                'Console.WriteLine(rdr("name"))
            Loop
            conn.Close()
            conn = New SqlConnection("Data Source=MSSERVER;
Initial Catalog=test;Integrated Security=True;Pooling=False")
            conn.Open()
            cmd = New SqlCommand("SQLCLRStudentCount", conn)
            Dim rowCount As Integer = cmd.ExecuteScalar
            conn.Close()
```

This has been a very brief overview of some of the features that are available using SQLCLR in SQL Server 2005 to run Visual Basic code on the SQL Server 2005 database server. For additional information, go to *www.msdn.com* and search for the article by Pablo Castro entitled "Managed Data Access Inside SQL Server with ADO.NET and SQLCLR." For purely tabular data, T-SQL will often perform faster than Visual Basic code running in SQLCLR. Examine the requirements of your application when deciding if T-SQL or Visual Basic and SQLCLR will be used.

Chapter Summary

ADO.NET 2.0 has a number of new features that make it easier to access and navigate data from databases:

- ADO.NET 2.0 and Visual Basic 2005 allow existing ADO.NET 1.0 code to run without change.
- Server Explorer and the Data Sources window allow access to databases to be easily configured.
- Drag-and-drop data access has been improved with than addition of a navigation control that allows a DataGridView to have rows inserted, deleted, and updated to reconcile these changes with the database.
- Drag-and-drop data access supports master-detail display of data.
- Provider factories can allow you to write code to access multiple databases such as Microsoft Access or Microsoft SQL Server using the same code.
- SQL Server 2005 SQLCLR allows you to run Visual Basic code in the form of stored procedures and user-defined functions on the database server.

ClickOnce Application Deployment

In this appendix you will:

- Discover how to use ClickOnce to publish an application
- Learn how to use ClickOnce to update an application
- Set configuration options to control ClickOnce application deployment

One of the reasons Web applications are popular is the ease with which they can be installed and updated. Chapter 4 covered some of advancements in ASP.NET 2.0. Microsoft has been working diligently to make it easier to install and especially update Windows Forms applications written using the .NET Framework. Microsoft's first attempt at making desktop applications easier to install and update was called No Touch Deployment. Visual Studio 2005 replaces No Touch Deployment with **ClickOnce** deployment. ClickOnce is built into Windows Forms projects in Visual Basic 2005. There is even a publishing wizard that makes ClickOnce deployment quite easy.

Application Publishing Wizard

Visual Studio 2005 includes an application publishing wizard that makes it easy to publish an application and publish updated versions of the application. This is a new feature in Visual Studio 2005. The following sections will walk you through how to initially publish your application. Once the application has been published, it can be installed from a URL or a network drive. The Updating an Application section describes how to publish and install updates to your application.

Publishing an Application

Once you have created a Visual Basic 2005 Windows Application, it can be deployed from Internet Information Server (IIS) using the Visual Studio 2005 Publishing Wizard. You can use the Publishing Wizard to publish your application using the following steps:

ClickOnce applications can be deployed using IIS or Universal Network Connection (UNC) drives that can be configured on any Windows System.

1. On the VS.NET menu, click **File**, then **New**, and then **Project**. Create a new Visual Basic 2005 Windows application named **ClickOnce**.
2. On the VS.NET menu, select **Build**, then click **Publish <*the name of your project*>**. Figure A-1 shows the Publishing Wizard. The application path includes the URL for the IIS Web server, and it then appends the name of the application, which in this case is **ClickOnce**. Click the **Next** button to advance the Publishing Wizard to the next step.

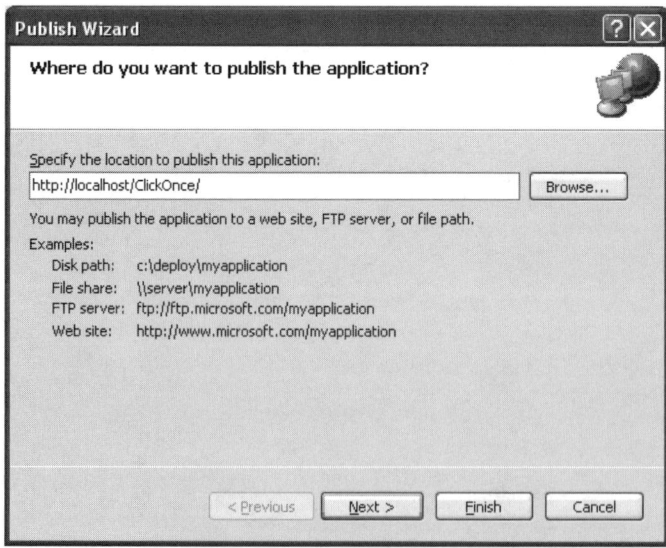

Figure A-1 The ClickOnce Publishing Wizard

3. The Publishing Wizard allows the selection of whether the application will be available both online and offline or online only, as shown in Figure A-2. If online or offline is selected, the application can be used with or without a network connection. If online is selected, the application can be used only when there is a live network connection. Click the **Next** button to advance the Publishing Wizard to the next step.

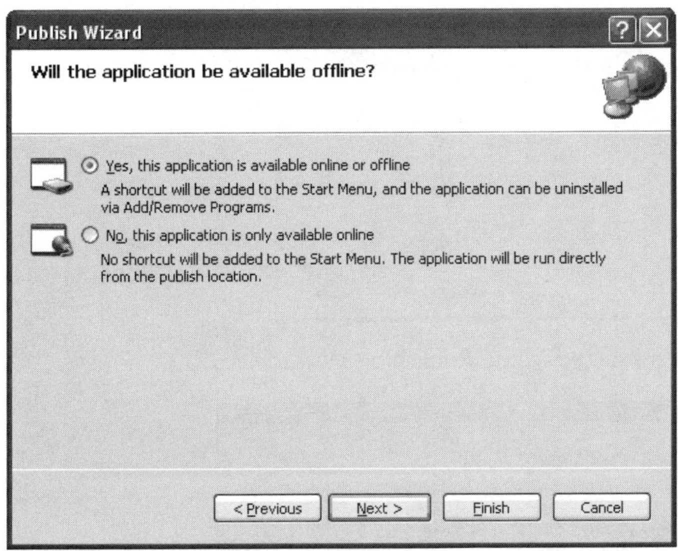

Figure A-2 Select whether the application will be available online

4. The Publishing Wizard in Figure A-3 shows the settings that have been selected so far. Click the **Finish** button to publish the application.
5. When the application has been published, Visual Studio 2005 automatically opens a Web page to allow the application to be installed, as shown in Figure A-4. To do so, click the **Install** button.

The URL remains the same for the application if you choose to update it. If you are planning to let others install the application, you should make sure they can access this Web page and provide them with the URL for installation.

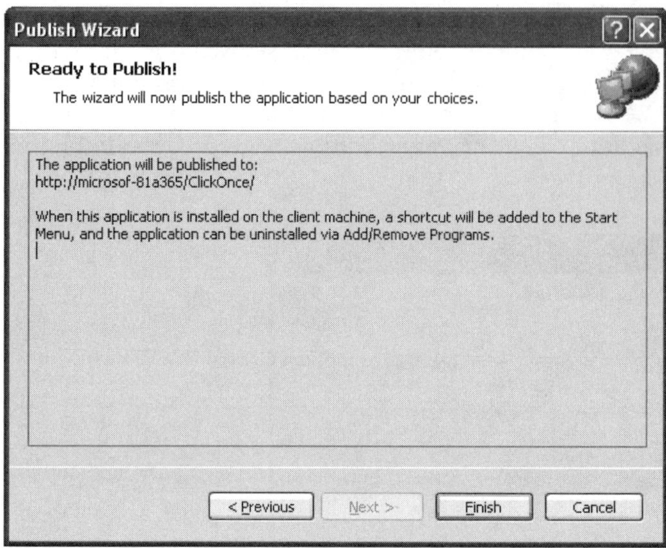

Figure A-3 The settings selected in the Publishing Wizard

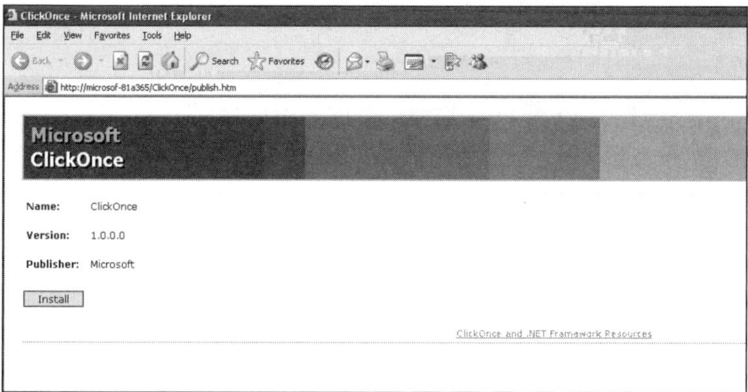

Figure A-4 ClickOnce-generated installation Web page

6. The Application Install – Security Warning dialog box is displayed if the application being installed is not signed, as shown in Figure A-5. In general this security warning should be taken quite seriously. Install software only when you know and trust the source of the software. Click the **More Information** link at the bottom right of the dialog box to display additional information about the security warning, as shown in Figure A-6. Click **OK** to return to the Application Install – Security Warning dialog box.

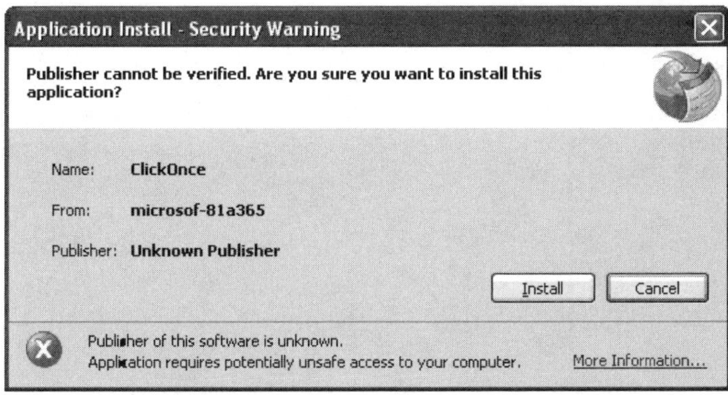

Figure A-5 Application Install - Security Warning: Unknown Publisher

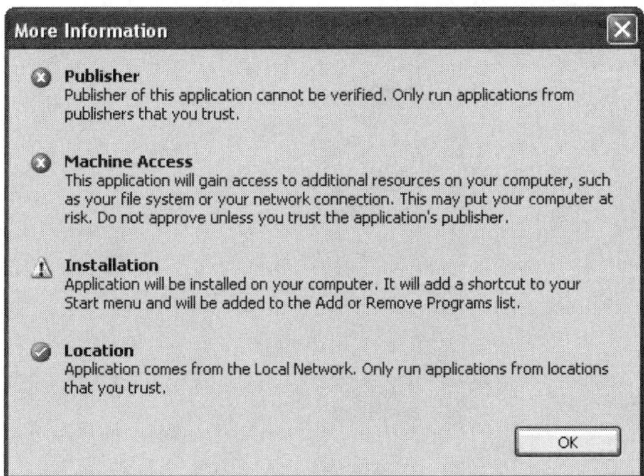

Figure A-6 More Information on the security warning

7. Because you are the publisher of this application, click **Install** to start the installation of this application, as shown in Figure A-7.

Once ClickOnce has installed the application, there are a couple of other tasks that are completed as well. First, the application is added to the choices available on the Windows Start menu, as shown in Figure A-8; second, the application is added to the Add or Remove Programs dialog box, as shown in Figure A-9. This allows the application to be uninstalled, if necessary.

Figure A-7 Your application is installed and started

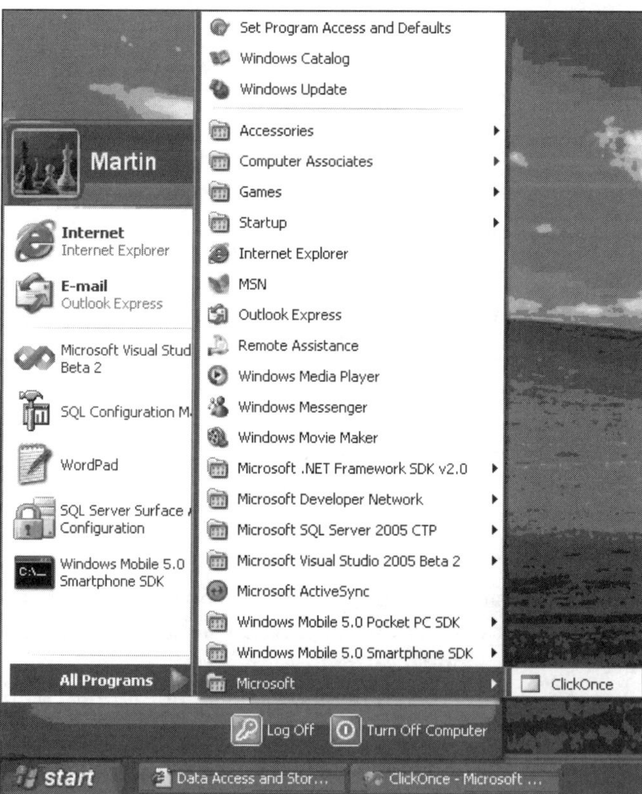

Figure A-8 The ClickOnce application is installed

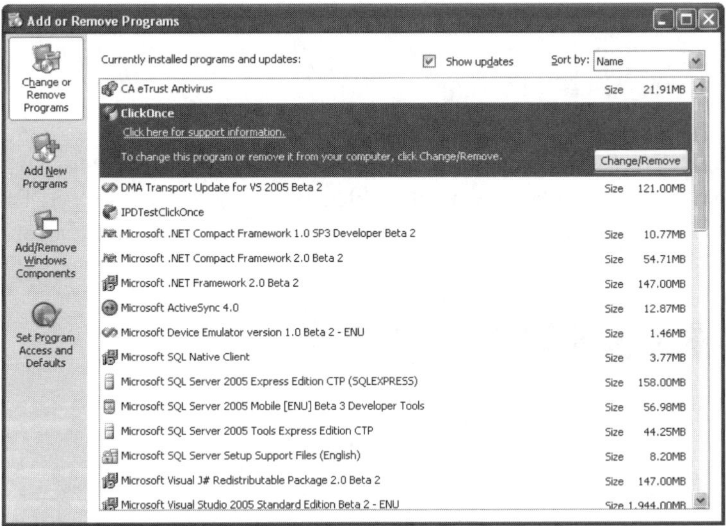

Figure A-9 The application is added to Add or Remove Programs

Updating an Application

Earlier it was mentioned that ClickOnce has two main goals. The first was to allow Windows Forms applications to be installed easily, and the second was so they could be updated easily. Currently, the application is simply an empty form. The following steps first update the application so the version number is displayed in the title bar, and then finish by republishing and reinstalling the application.

1. Open **Form1.vb** in the Design view.
2. Double-click the form to open the **Form_Load** event and add the following code:

```
Try
    If (My.Application.IsNetworkDeployed) Then
        Me.Text = _
             My.Application.Deployment.CurrentVersion._
ToString()
    End If
Catch ex As Exception
    MessageBox.
Show("This application needs to be published", "Error")
End Try
```

3. On the VS 2005 menu, click **Build**, then click **Publish ClickOnce**. The Publishing Wizard is displayed.

4. Click **Finish** to publish the application. The installation Web page is displayed. Note the version number is now 1.0.0.1. Close the browser. Instead of installing the application, you will run the application and let the application discover that a new version exists.

5. Click the **Windows Start** button, then click **All Programs**, **Microsoft**, and then click **ClickOnce**. The Update Available dialog box opens, as shown in Figure A-10. Click **OK**. If you click **Skip**, the current version of the application is still available for use.

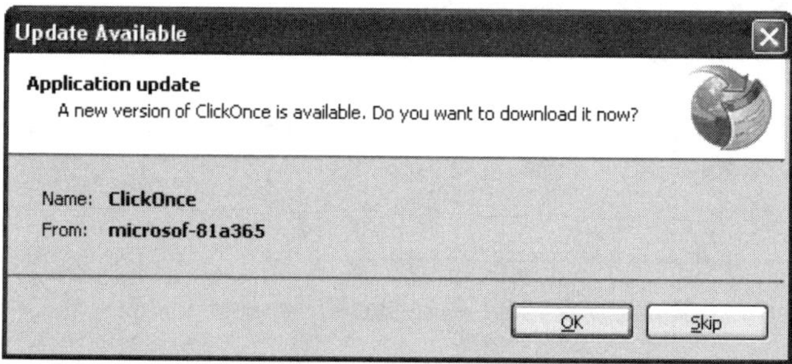

Figure A-10 A newer version of the application exists

6. The 1.0.0.1 version of ClickOnce has been deployed, as shown in Figure A-11.

Figure A-11 The updated ClickOnce application

If you are notified that a new version exists, but after installation find you are running an older version, it could be caused by file caching by the Web server or a router.

Once an application has been updated, there is a fallback position should the new application not work correctly. By going to Control Panel and selecting Add or Remove Programs, as shown in Figure A-9, the application can be rolled back to the previous version. By clicking the Change/Remove button, the ClickOnce Maintenance dialog is displayed, as shown in Figure A-12. This dialog box allows the application to be removed or restored to the previous version.

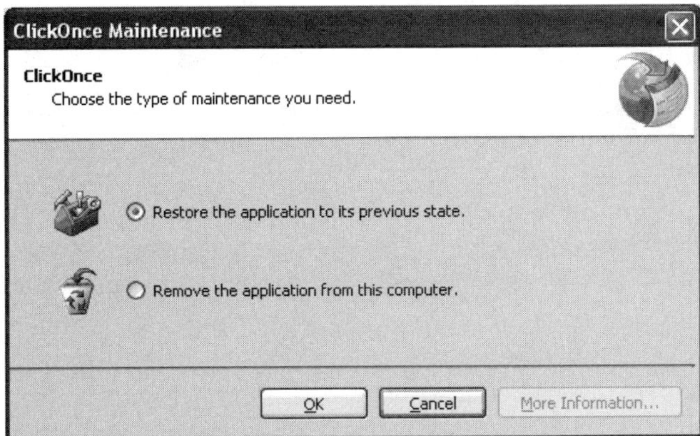

Figure A-12 ClickOnce Maintenance dialog box

Configuration Options for ClickOnce Applications

There are a number of configuration options that are available for ClickOnce applications. By accessing the properties for the project ClickOnce applications, settings can be modified. Application properties can be accessed by clicking View, Solution Explorer, right-clicking on the project, and then clicking Open from the context menu, as shown in Figure A-13.

Once application properties are displayed, clicking on the Publish tab displays settings for ClickOnce applications, as shown in Figure A-14. Figure A-15 shows the publishing options available after the Options button in Figure A-14 is clicked. You may have noticed in Figure A-8 that the desktop folder that contained the application was labeled *Microsoft*. This is because the default value for publisher is *Microsoft*. In the Publish Options dialog box, changing the publisher name causes the application install folder to use the specified publisher name.

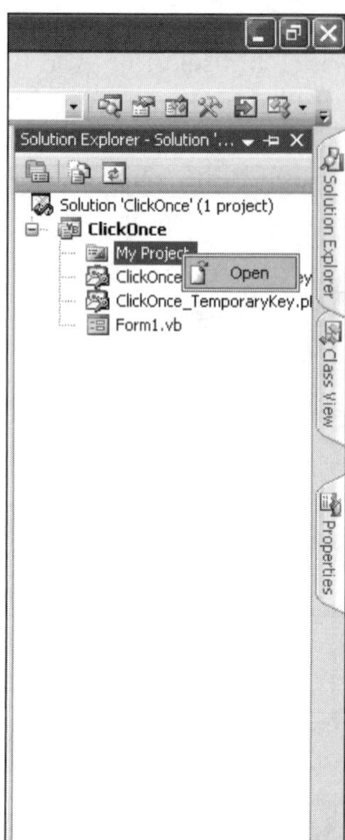

Figure A-13 Accessing the Project properties

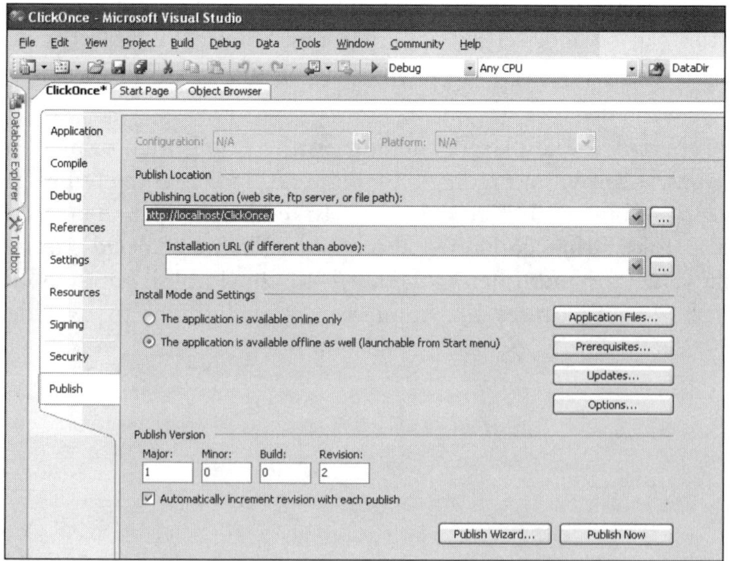

Figure A-14 Application properties, Publish tab

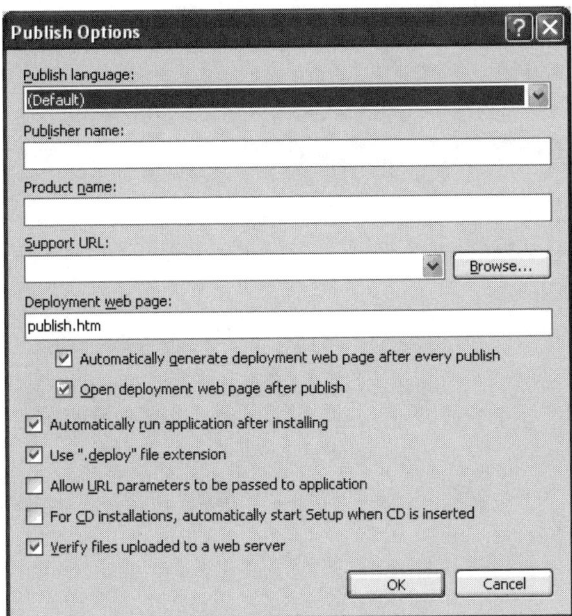

Figure A-15 Useful Publish Options

Summary

- ClickOnce allows Windows Forms applications to be packaged for easy installation using the Application Publish Wizard.
- ClickOnce makes installing a Windows Forms application easy.
- ClickOnce allows deployed applications to be updated easily.
- There are a large number of configuration options that allow ClickOnce to be tailored to your needs.

Index

B

C

E